Recollections of the Peninsula

Recollections of the Peninsula

An Officer of the 34th Regiment of Foot—
'The Cumberland Gentlemen'—on
Campaign Against Napoleon's
French Army in Spain

Moyle Sherer

LEONAUR

*Recollections of the Peninsula: an Officer of the 34th Regiment of Foot—
'The Cumberland Gentlemen'—on Campaign Against Napoleon's
French Army in Spain*
by Moyle Sherer

Originally published under the title
Recollections of the Peninsula

Published by Leonaur Ltd

Text in this form and material original to this edition
copyright © 2008 Leonaur Ltd

ISBN: 978-1-84677-512-3 (hardcover)
ISBN: 978-1-84677-511-6 (softcover)

http://www.leonaur.com

Contents

Preface

The following pages have occupied and amused the leisure of my winter evenings, in a dull uninteresting garrison on home service. I relate what I saw, thought, and felt, as a man, a traveller, and a soldier, during five interesting years.

The style of a soldier can need no apology; it is beneath the notice of a scholar and the critic. We pass our lives in conversing with mankind; they in conversing with books. We only observe and draw hasty conclusions; they observe, compare, and study. Ours is a life of action; theirs of repose. We write to amuse; they to instruct.

CHAPTER 1

Lisbon

He, to whom the interest of foreign scenes, the animation of the daily march, and the careless gaiety of camps are familiar, may be expected to languish in the solitude of a barrack-room, and to feel restless at a life of dull and wearisome inaction. Accustomed to the array of thousands, he turns with indifference from the parade of a regiment; nor can the ordinary duties of a quiet garrison be supposed to satisfy him who has served with armies in the field. The life of a soldier abroad is one of foreign travel, as well as of active employment; and it combines, therefore, rational enjoyment with honourable service. The campaigns of the British army in Spain, had peculiarly that character; for we moved over large tracts of country, and our operations were not, as is often the case in war, confined to marches and counter-marches in particular districts. The British soldiers, who landed on the banks of the Tagus, visited, in succession, those of the Douro, the Ebro, and the Bidassoa; were encamped under the walls of Madrid, and bivouacked on the Pyrenean mountains. In those scenes, and on that service, many of us experienced feelings of contentment, joy, and pride, for the return of which we may look, perhaps, in vain. At the distance of time at which I write, all that was disagreeable in campaigning is forgotten; while that which delighted, is, especially in my present frame of mind, very fondly remembered.

The unpretending volume I offer is not copious; but the few anecdotes I relate are true, the military sketches are faithful, and my descriptions of towns and scenery are, with all their imperfections, at least my own. For the reflections, opinions, and warm (perhaps romantic) expressions of feeling I have scattered through these pages, they are such as naturally arose to me, both as a soldier and a man.

It was in the last week of June, 1809, that I embarked at Portsmouth, to follow and join my regiment, which had already sailed for Portugal. On the tenth morning after my departure from England, the vessel which bore me was passing under the rock of Lisbon, impelled by a favourable breeze, and she in a very few hours dropped her anchor in the harbour of Lisbon, nearly abreast of Belem Castle, and about a mile from the shore. Few scenes can compare with that which feasts the eye of a traveller, who, from the deck of a vessel in the Tagus, first gazes on Lisbon, rising proudly and beautifully above him. The northern bank of the river on which this capital is built, makes a handsome and sweeping curve throughout the whole extent of the city, which, including its suburbs, covers several hills, rising more or less abruptly from that quarter where its quays, squares, and some of its most regular streets are conveniently disposed. The number of palaces, convents, and churches, which crown this amphitheatre of buildings; the dazzling whiteness of the houses; the light appearance of the windows and balconies; the tasteful arrangement of plants, flowers, and shrubs on their roofs and terraces; the golden orange-groves which adorn the suburbs; and the stately specimens of Indian or American botany, which are, here. and there, scattered through the scene, produce an effect which may be felt, and which may be conceived, but which cannot be described.

Boats from the shore soon crowded round our vessel, and I leaned over her side to look, for the first time, at natives of Portugal. The dark-brown complexion, bare and muscular throat, expressive eye, and white teeth, together with the general vivacity of their deportment, strike an Englishman, at first, very forcibly: their costume, too, is quite new to him, and I think, very picturesque. Short petticoat-trowsers of white linen, a red sash, and their legs and arms free and naked, mark very strongly the difference between the boatmen of the Tagus and the Thames.

The British troops at Lisbon were at this time all encamped in the Prince's Park, a large enclosure above the suburb of Belem, carefully preserved. In an old ruined house, the only building in or near the encampment, the mess of my regiment still held its social sittings; and here, found a rudely constructed table of casks and planks, seated on portmanteaus, stones, or knapsacks, we enjoyed our evening far more than we had often done at a board better provided, and in the most commodious mess-room. The conversation no longer ran in the same dull, unvarying strain, on scenes of expensive folly and fatiguing amusement; the dignity of our profession, which will naturally in such scenes glide from the view, again rose before us, arrayed in its best and brightest colours. New prospects and eager hopes gave an animation and interest to the discourse, which, seasoned as it was by some excellent wine, made time fly swiftly, and it was midnight before I entered my tent Here a couch of heath, freshly gathered, with my knapsack for a pillow, and a blanket for a covering, invited me to repose; but I was far too happy to sleep.

The night was hot: I opened the door of my tent, raised all the walls, and throwing myself on my bed of heather, I indulged in waking dreams. We can only command the services of sleep when we are contented or weary; but when our happiness arises from the prospect of still greater enjoyment, the mind is too active for slumber, and the very body becomes restless. At four in the morning I refreshed myself with dressing, leisurely, in the open air; and at five the corps was under arms, to be inspected by General Catlin Crawford.

One thousand and seventy bayonets, all fine-sized, efficient men, then mustered under our colours. My regiment has never been very roughly handled in the field, although it has borne handsome share of honourable peril. But, alas! what between; sickness, suffering, and the sword, few, very few of those men are now in existence. We had yearly supplies of men from the depôt; they too have for the most part disappeared.

Our inspection over, I set forth, with some companions, to devote a day to Lisbon. We passed from the bridge of Alcantara, by one continued street, through the, suburbs, to the city.

The appearance of every thing around me was so totally novel, that it is impossible for me to describe the singular, yet pleasing impression produced on my mind. To find myself walking amid a concourse of people, differing in feature, complexion and dress, so widely from the natives of England; to hear, the continued sound of a language I could not understand; and to find myself, though a youthful foreigner, an object of notice and respect, as a British officer, was at once strange; and delightful. The picturesque dress of the common, peasants, the long strings of loaded mules, the cabriolets; the bullock-cars, as rude and ancient in their construction, as those in the frontispiece to the Georgics of the oldest Virgils; the water-carriers; the lemonade-sellers; and, above all, the monks and friars in the habits of their orders: the style of the houses, the handsome entrances, the elegant balconies, the rare and beautiful plants arranged in them, all raised around me a scene which, real as it was, seemed almost the deception of a theatre.

In the small square of San Paulo, we stopped, and breakfasted in a light, cheerful room, which looked out on the quay. Here, while sipping my coffee, I commanded a view of the noble harbour, crowded with vessels; while many pilot and fishing barks, with their large, handsome Latin sails, were coming up or going down the river; and, nearer the shore, hundreds of small neat boats, with white or painted awnings, were transporting passengers from one quay to another, or to the more distant suburbs of Alcantara and Belem. The whole of this picture was lighted up by a sun, such as is only to be met with in a southern climate, and so bright, that it appeared to animate every thing on which it shone. Immediately under the window of our café, some Moorish porters, of whom there are many in Lisbon, were occupied in their surprising labours.

Their Herculean frames, small turbans, and striking features, and their prodigious exertions in lifting and carrying immense and weighty packages, presented us with a new and uncommon scene. My mind naturally reverted to that era in past ages, when these Moormen, now so degraded, and, politically considered, so insignificant, swayed the sceptre of this beauteous land, and when, from the very source to the mouth of the golden Tagus, the crescent was triumphantly displayed.

We proceeded, immediately after breakfast, to take a survey of the city; and ascending a very steep, though well-built street, made our way to the church of San Roque. My attention was arrested in passing the magnificent house, or rather palace, of the Baron Quintella, by the sight of one of those large groups of beggars, so common in this country. Round the gateway, and under the walls of this mansion, they lay, indolently stretched out, and only implored our charity by extending the hand. To follow, and importune us, was an exertion they never dreamed of; and in this last particular, they must be allowed to irritate a passenger far less, than the sturdy beggars occasionally met with in London, and the more numerous swarms, which infest half the towns in Ireland.

In the southern countries of Europe, openly professing the Roman Catholic religion, the giving of alms is considered an imperative duty; and according to their means, all persons supply the wants of the necessitous. From the gates of the convents, from the kitchens of the wealthy, food is daily distributed to a certain number of mendicants; and there is no person, however humble his condition, if he be above want, who does not give a something, in charity, every day of his life. Hence, secure of the means to support their wretched existence, they betake themselves daily to their respective stations, await the summons from the porter of the monastery, or the palace; and thankfully receive the small coin of the casual passenger. It is true, that such scenes are painful; but we must learn the cause of them before we abuse the nation, by which they are, presented.

Without poor laws, or poor rates, without workhouses, or any parish institutions, these beggars are, of necessity, exposed to public view, and supported in the eye of day. The numbers of those who subsist, on public charity in Portugal, as compared even with our own country, would not be found so great as we might at first imagine; and, indeed, in their mild climate, and with their peculiar habits, these unfortunate paupers might, after all, gain little in real happiness, by the introduction of poor houses and parish, officers.

We entered the church of San Roque just as the consecrated wafer was held up to view. The low bending posture of a vast congregation, all of whom were on their knees, and most of whom beat their breasts fervently with their hands, quite startled me, and I bent my head, with mingled feelings of reverence and shame. These, however, were soon dispelled; for when this crowd rose to depart, I could see no trace on their features of serious impression; they all entered into condensation with vivacity and eagerness, and the ladies threw their brilliant eyes around them, with all the consciousness of their power. Many of the ladies were followed by black female servants, and some by superior attendants of a certain age, who had all the appearance of, and were, I believe, *duennas*.

When the church was cleared, we walked slowly round it. It was spacious and handsome: the shrines were rich, but not so overloaded with gilding as many I afterwards saw. The decorations of the high altar were not remarkable; but a finely executed mosaic, over one of the side altars, representing the baptism of our Saviour by St John, was at once a most curious and beautiful specimen of art. I have never seen any mosaic work since, half so delicate, or, indeed, at all to be compared with it.

At a large fountain in this neighbourhood we stopped for a moment, to view the patient and industrious Gallegos, who, provided with small wooden barrels, supply all the citizens with water, at a trifling cost. These men are natives of the distant province of Gallicia, in Spain; they pass the best of their days in this city, and in this humble occupation; and return with their small savings to repose in the country which gave them birth, when, through age or infirmity, they are no longer able to work; There are, also, many Gallicians in Lisbon, who act as porters and servants, and they bear a very high character for honesty and fidelity.

In the course of our walk we visited all the best parts of the city. The *Rocio*, or square of the Inquisition, is a fine spacious place; and near the palace of that tribunal, the destructive influence of which, I learned with pleasure, had been very greatly, repressed, a large detachment of the police guards, both horse and foot, were parading: their costume, appointments, and, in fact, their whole appearance was soldier-like and imposing. While attentively observing them, I was not a little surprised to see the cavalry dismount, the infantry present arms, and then the whole, on one knee, with their heads bare, join as in an act of devotion. On turning round, I perceived the procession of the host passing across the square, and all the multitude that filled it was kneeling, motionless, and uncovered.

Not far from hence, in an open space near the gardens of the Salitre, a fair or market for the sale of horses is often held. The contrast between this scene and a horse-fair in England is great indeed: the small size, long tails, and flowing manes of the Portuguese horses; their paces, either a slow prancing amble, or a high short gallop; and the clumsiness and singularity of their horse furniture and saddlery;—strike an Englishman at first very forcibly. The collars of their mules are of worsted, of the most curious patterns, of all colours, and generally ornamented with bells. The head-stalls and reins of their riding-horses are all studded with brass ornaments, and the saddles are heavy wooden frames, covered with buff leather, soft, and padded, and having on the pummel and cant two high projections, so contrived as to wedge in the rider. Their stirrup is the large wooden one, covering the foot, and the very same which was used four centuries ago.[1]

From the horse-fair we passed into the garden of the Salitre: it is small, but affords a cool and shady promenade. Returning by the *Rocio*, we walked to the Commercial square, which is truly handsome, and very regularly built. One front of it is open to the

---

1. The Portuguese gentlemen have, however, latterly adopted the saddles of English form, and in many things now imitate the; English closely.

15

river, and large and convenient flights of stone steps descend to the very edge of the water. A lofty *piazza* runs round two sides of it, and here the merchants meet to learn the news of the day, and transact the business of the exchange. In the centre is a fine equestrian statue of John the Great, in bronze. Three very well-built, uniform streets, communicate between this square and that of the Inquisition: one wholly filled with the shops of gold jewellers and lapidaries, another by silversmiths, and a third by cloth-merchants and embroiderers. The shops are small, and the windows have a singular appearance, looking like square glass cases, detached and placed outside for show. The accommodations in the houses above these shops. are excellent, each family here, as in Paris, occupying a separate floor.

I purchased some trinkets in Gold Street cheap, and very elegant. Their chain-work is delicate, and their crosses have a character, both as to form and setting, very peculiar, and I think tasteful. We next visited the castle, and the convent of St. Vincent The former is certainly not remarkable for any thing but its site; and the soldiers on duty had nothing martial in their carriage and appearance. I have always a mingled and undefined feeling of pride and humiliation, when I reflect on what discipline can do towards the formation of an army; I say humiliation, because the well-organised bands of a despot can, by skilful dispositions and unity of effort, always defeat numbers vastly superior, of men, animated, perhaps, by the purest patriotism that ever warmed or ennobled the heart, but unassisted by a practical acquaintance with war. I feel proud, however, to think, that by the discipline we gave, to second the courage they never wanted, the Portuguese were enabled to repel their unprincipled invaders; and, by the side of our own gallant troops, to carry the white standard of their country into the fertile region of southern France,

At the convent of St. Vincent we were received with the most flattering politeness. The good fathers presented us with fruit and wine, and showed us the building, with an eagerness, perhaps, not wholly free from pride. Their apartments, though very plainly furnished, were exceedingly comfortable; and all of them opened into a long spacious gallery, at the extremity of which a large window commanded a view of that ever-varying and ever-beautiful scene, the harbour of Lisbon. Their church was splendidly adorned: the holy vessels, for the service of the altar, rich and sumptuous; the organ fine, but singular in its construction, the pipes being arranged horizontally. The vestments for the use of the officiating priests were truly magnificent. They had a small garden, well laid out, and prettily embellished with fountains and busts. Most of the monks here are well born, and educated with some care. They spoke highly of our nation, and of the late successes of Wellington (then Sir Arthur Wellesley) in the north of Portugal, and they asked many intelligent questions about the army,

We departed, pleased with our cordial reception, and not a little surprised at the comfort in which these holy brethren lived. This was the first convent I had ever seen; nor could I find it in my heart to apply to its inmates the contemptuous epithets with which they are too often branded. While I regret that any government, or religion, should condemn so many of its members to a life of cheerless celibacy and useless devotion, I am far from despising, or even: blaming, the unhappy victims of ecclesiastical policy and pride: for, believe me, the discipline of the wealthiest orders is sufficiently austere to shut out all those enjoyments of life which are so generally and so highly prized ; and there are few if any of us, who rail at monks, who could consent, even from a sense of duty, to lead the insipid and wearisome lives of those unhappy men.

On our way back to. the Largo de San Paulo, where we dined, I entered many of their churches, but there was in general little to admire. The decorations were in a tawdry and offensive taste; and a profusion of badly-executed carved work, gilt and painted, quite fatigued the eye. One custom of this, and I believe, all Catholic countries, delighted me: at all hours the gates of the churches stand open, and in them, at all hours, may be seen some individuals pouring forth their hearts in prayer at the shrines of their respective saints. In the hour of affliction, distress, or ter-

17

ror, hither they come; and here, protected and assisted by the holiness and solemnity of the place, they repose their sorrows and their fears in the bosom of their God, and invoke his mercy and forgiveness. How many a prostrate penitent have I seen, too much absorbed in his devotions to cast one hasty glance of curiosity around him, disturbed as he must have been by my approach! Oh! there are, I believe, moments in the life of every man, when to fly to a consecrated temple, and to throw himself at the foot of the altar, unsummoned by any bell for prayers, but urged solely by the tone of his mind, and the overflowing of his heart, must be felt as a pure and a holy pleasure.

Occupied in such reflections, I walked slowly behind my companions, when suddenly raising my eyes, they had disappeared. Several persons, with ready and natural politeness, by voice and gesture, directed me and I followed them through the gates of the arsenal. Here we remained a very short time; for to the eyes of Englishmen, although the building was fine, the docks and yard appeared rather those of a private ship-builder, than the grand naval depôt of a nation. Yet it was impossible to forget, that this nation had equipped and sent forth the vessel which bore the enterprising Vasco de Gama, and that her mariners were the first who found and followed that path over the trackless ocean to India, which has since been ploughed by so many keels, freighted with European avarice and ambition.

At our dinner, which was served at an hotel kept by a Frenchman, I found some of our party had been very differently impressed with the morning's ramble to what I had been. They drew comparisons between London and Lisbon exultingly, without reflecting that it was impossible to do this fairly. Where I had been struck by the fine appearance of some public building, or private palace, they had only seen the heaps of dirt lying near the portals;—where I had gazed, with pleasure, on some diversified groups of market peasantry, in their national costume, they had discovered a squalid beggar mingling in the crowd;—while I had seen some expressive face, lean over a balcony, on one side of the street, and had inhaled the perfume of some rich and powerful exotics, they, on the other, had encountered a fish-woman frying *sardinias* at her stall, or been saluted by some unfortunate puff of air, impregnated with garlic:— with such different eyes do men look upon the same scenes.[2]

I am sure that I should approach, and gaze upon it tomorrow, with an admiration very little chilled or weakened by long years of travel, or by the fixedly impressed aspect of many scenes of a different, and (I admit in some few instances) of a superior beauty; but I cannot, will not plead guilty to the clothing of, "really disgusting realities in the garb of enchantment;" had I the ability to perform this miracle, I should be wanting in inclination. Alas! the realities this lady speaks of, are of a nature rather to humiliate, and depress. The dirty shirt, the uncombed hair, the scratching search, the ash-heap, the offal, the ordure and the puddle, and the open shameless sacrifice to Cloacina; these things are found in Naples, in Rome, in Venice, aye, and in the corners of all cities, where there is much want, and no hope. Indolence is the besetting sin of all southern nations; dirt is the offspring of indolence; despotic princes and lazy priests are most encouraging godfathers of the ragged bantling. I must be pardoned for smiling at the notion, that the officers of Wellington's army, who were literally, in many instances, domesticated among the people (of all classes) had unfavourable opportunities for observing on the manners and customs of the Portuguese nation compared to this amiable and animated lady, whose seclusion and confinement in a city so very unsocial, we quite mourn over as we read of it. As to Mr. Matthews, if he had opened his moral eye a little

---

2. In the Preface to a late work on Lisbon, in two small volumes, by a lady, I find these few pages of mine noticed in such a manner, that the reproach of the disappointed traveller, although conveyed in language, and with a turn of compliment the most flattering, is sufficiently apparent. It is now fifteen years since I first visited the city of Lisbon; twelve since I last looked upon it; eight since I penned this short, and hurried description—a recollection indeed—a *mere* recollection, but a faithful picture of what I should expect to see again, if I sailed for the Tagus tomorrow. True it is, there are many things in Lisbon "unsightly to strange e'e, (For hut and palace show 'like filthily, The dingy denizens are reared in dirt;") but after all it is a city, "that sheening far, celestial seems to be."

19

wider in Lisbon, during his three weeks sojourn, his numerous and admiring readers would have thanked him. In the very few remarks he has offered on the state of society there, he has fallen into one or two most unaccountable errors. I must also observe, that the taste of that sensible and well-informed gentleman is not easily warmed into admiration. See his remarks on *the Genius and Merits of Michael Angelo*, and his cold *Promenade through the noble Collection of Statues in the Museo Borbonico at Naples*.

After contriving to make a very excellent meal, in spite of the clamours of my companions at the style of the cookery, and the manner of serving up the dinner, I went with one of them to the theatre, in the Rua das Condes.

The action of the performers, though vulgar, was sufficiently expressive to give mean insight into the comedy they represented; the subject of it was very droll, and not unlike our "Beggar's Opera." To the play succeeded a tolerable ballet: a Madame Brunet, a handsome woman, and a graceful dancer, formed the chief attraction of it. There was also a grotesque, or comic dance, executed by four clumsy-looking men, whose activity was nevertheless truly surprising, and very loudly applauded by the spectators. The form of this house is ugly and. ill-contrived, being narrow and long; and the stage too, though sufficiently deep, has no width. The sound of the Portuguese language is very unpleasing to foreigners, from the nasal tone. The instrumental music, however, in their orchestra, is excellent.

Here, as in other parts of the continent, ladies do not dress for the theatre. I saw some very pretty women, who seemed, by the way, infinitely more diverted with watching the effects of the representation on us Englishmen, than the performance itself. The Portuguese have often been described by travellers as being very negligent about their persons, and very dirty in their dress and appearance. I confess I did not find them so; on the contrary, I had occasion to remark, that all the middling and upper classes of society were very particular, both as to the fineness and whiteness of their linen. The middle-sized plump form, black, bright, and expressive eyes and regular teeth of a dazzling whiteness, are the peculiar characteristics of the beauty of a Portuguese female, and constitute here, as they would any where else, a very pretty woman. Neither is the stature of the men in Lisbon, though certainly lower than that of Englishmen, so diminutive as it has been often, and very falsely, represented.

My friend and I parted at the door of the theatre, and after taking an ice at the Grotto, a very excellent coffee-room in the Largo de San Paulo, much frequented by English and Americans, I threw myself into one of the small boats constantly plying here, and protected: by an awning from the heavy dew, was rowed swiftly, to a landing-place below Alcantara, and not very distant from our camp. It was past the hour of midnight when I left Lisbon, and the most perfect stillness reigned in the crowded harbour, save here and there at intervals the bells striking the hour, or the hoarse voice of some seamen challenging the passing boat, whose gently splashing oars were faintly heard.

There is something inexpressibly soothing in the sensations we experience at such an hour, and in such a scene. Its effect on me was too delightful to be ever forgotten. In passing very near the garden of a handsome residence, in which lights were yet burning, my ear caught the sound of music I bade my boatmen rest upon their oars, and distinctly heard a very beautiful air, sung by a sweet female voice, and accompanied by the guitar.

I thought of England for one short moment with a sigh, and with all that heaviness of heart which a youth alone can feel, and which youthful spirits alone can conquer. The rapidly following challenges of the British sentinels first awoke me from the reverie into which this invisible siren had thrown me, and hurrying to my tent, alike pleased with my day, and exhausted by fatigue, I threw myself, dressed as I was, upon my bed of heath, and slept profoundly.

CHAPTER 2

Marching Through Portugal

The whole of the next day I was confined by duty to the lines of the encampment; I found my Portuguese grammar the best company possible. The first principles of grammar are every where the same, and as Latin is the ground-work of both the languages spoken in the Peninsula, I found my studies rather amusing than laborious. I suffered no peasant, muleteer, or fruit-woman to pass the door of my tent unquestioned, and by paying very particular attention to their mariner and tone, I was soon enabled to make my own wants and enquiries intelligible, and to comprehend their replies. Charles the Fifth has wisely observed, the more languages a man can speak, the more frequently does he feel himself a man; a remark founded on a close observation of human nature. The pride of a man of any intellect receives a severe wound, when he is first thrown into a circle of foreigners, whose conversation he cannot understand. His very features lose their ordinary intelligence, and, like a deaf man in a crowded and brilliant assembly, he wears the eager look of restless and mortified anxiety, or the more painful gaze of cheerless and vacant stupidity. To a military man, some acquaintance with the language of the country, which, is the theatre of war, is almost indispensable, and a more intimate knowledge of it, if it does not prove, as it often has done, an introduction to notice, and a ready and creditable channel to professional distinction, will be a constant source of satisfaction, pleasure, and advantage. Though daily expecting a route, our column remained nearly a month in this camp. Between visits to Lisbon and Belem, and daily walks in the neighbourhood, the whole of this time to me passed very delightfully.

I regretted, in common with others, the arrangement which delayed us at Lisbon, while we panted to be marching in advance; but to consume time uselessly by thinking and talking of what I had not the power to remedy, was never in my nature. Besides, there was too much variety and novelty all around me, for any feeling of tedium and discontent to dwell long in my bosom. Today I would indulge in the unaccustomed pleasure of wandering in a spacious orange-grove, or seated by some garden fountain, under the shade of a luxuriant fig-tree, learn my self-prescribed lesson in Portuguese, while some smiling labourer would place the choicest fruit at my feet, resisting any attempt of mine to reward him, with such sayings as, "They are my master's; he is hospitable and generous."

"God gives enough for all."

"You are the brave English, our allies: if you were not here to fight for us, stranger hands might reap our corn, and spoil our vineyards."

Another morning I would go and explore what I had left unseen. At Belem there is a Royal Museum, small indeed, but well selected. It is indebted for its principal curiosities to South America and India.

There is, or rather was, a menagerie in the king's garden, for at the time I saw it, it contained nothing remarkable. In the garden are a few shady walks, but nothing like space, variety, or arrangement. Near it stands a large unfinished palace, of the finest masonry, and built on a scale far more magnificent than any thing to be met with in England. I walked, however, through the long suit of lofty chambers with very little gratification, and felt that comfort was never likely to be an inmate there. This same comfort, the household god of the English gentleman, is unknown on the Continent, and never consents to dwell amid marble pillars, polished mirrors, and gilt furniture. The convent of White Friars at Belem is a noble Gothic building; its handsome and vaulted cloisters, beautiful garden, spacious galleries, and convenient chambers, all bespeak opulence.

The grand entrance of its church is highly and curiously ornamented in sculptured stone. The decorations of the interior correspond most fully. The shrines, the high altar, the choir, the organ, are all rich, yet elegantly so. Four large sarcophagi of marble, containing the ashes of buried royalty, are placed on either side of the church, not very distant from the high altar, and produce a fine and solemn effect. The good father who accompanied me, a venerable old man of seventy, had been nearly half a century a brother of the order, and an inmate of the convent. He had seen it, he told me, in the day of its glory, when it boasted a numerous and respected brotherhood. It was now, he said, losing members, property, and influence daily; he pointed out the stone to me under which he prayed to rest his bones, and told me he hoped that the blessing of death might not long be withheld. While he spoke to me, the tears trembled in his aged eyes, and I could not control a strong expression of sympathy, which at the moment I sincerely felt. On reflection, however, reason and humanity bade me rejoice. Perhaps we owe, even to the armies of the ambitious Napoleon, one blessing. Ecclesiastical government, monastic pride, and the withering tyranny of the priesthood, have shrunk before them; and though I hear it daily asserted, that the priests in the Peninsula again exercise their baleful influence over the liberty and the happiness of the people, still I am convinced that the authority of the church in Spain and Portugal has received a blow, from the effects of which it can never perfectly recover. The seeds of a new, and a better order of things have been sown, and though weeds may for a time obstruct their growth, that speculative and daring hand which cleans the encumbered soil, will reap an abundant and a healthy harvest. At some distance from these walls was a small convent of Irish nuns: it is not very richly endowed nor are the sisters many in number. I spoke with some of them, but cannot say that I felt half the interest I should wish to have deceived myself into feeling, at the grate of a nunnery.

One of the noviciates was certainly pretty; she asked me, with great innocence, if I did not admire Pope's Epistle from Eloisa to Abelard; said that she thought it beautiful; and that she was indebted to an English officer, who had kindly lent her a volume of poetry, for the perusal of this poem and others. I left her, not without some emotion of pity, for I thought that the man who had lent her the book of which she spoke, ought at least to have accompanied it with a ladder of ropes, and a promise of assistance and protection. Some evenings I would take a boat and row about the harbour, in order to catch views of the city from different points; others, I walked into Lisbon to look around me, or to make some trifling purchase, but not a day passed without enjoyment. I went frequently to the convent of the Estrella to hear the service. The church is most beautiful; the building exquisitely finished; and the interior chastely ornamented. A very elegant and well-proportioned dome, plain handsome altars, adorned with very tolerable paintings, the finest masonry, and a profusion of rich marble, call forth the admiration of all strangers. The service is always decently and solemnly performed, and the soft melodious voices of some of these nuns, as they chaunt the responses, or sing the anthem, touch the very soul.

I often returned from this service alone, and walked slowly back to the camp, by an unfrequented path-way, which passes exactly under the grand arch of the famous Lisbon aqueduct This noble arch, the chief wonder, and beauty of this magnificent work, is 340 feet in height, by about 240 in breadth, or span. The sight of an aqueduct carries with it, to the mind of an Englishman, impressions altogether new. It is a work of utility and grandeur, of which he has read in ancient history, and in travels, but which he prides himself to consider the advancement of science has rendered in most cases useless, and he is therefore ill prepared to waste any admiration on such a work, especially where it is not hallowed by antiquity; but when such an arch, as that of which I speak, first meets his eye, he; is struck with astonishment and awe; it appears as a proud monument of the power of man, a record of the prodigious labours which man, living in social and happy union with his fellow man, can effect.

I was very anxious, before we marched, to visit Cintra, a spot celebrated by all travellers, and proverbial with the inhabitants of Lisbon, for its romantic beauty. Our party, consisting of six, having obtained leave for two days, left the encampment at four o'clock one morning, in three decent cabriolets, and after a slow, but pleasant drive of two hours, reached Caluz, a summer palace of the queen's, with a small town attached. The country through which we passed to Caluz presented nothing in its appearance remarkable, if I except some fields of Indian corn, and some hedges, formed by American aloes of prodigious size, and uncommon beauty. The prickly pear, a very hideous plant, was here and there scattered among them. At Caluz, we visited the palace; the building is not fine, and the apartments are neither magnificently or elegantly decorated; there are, indeed, some very handsome mirrors, but the furniture, in general, is in a tawdry and wretched taste. The garden well suits the character of the palace; it is laid out in a formal, quaint style, trees, hedges, and box, being tortured into every possible variety of shape. Some clumsy statues, defaced busts, and ill-designed fountains, complete the picture.

We hastened back to our coffee, and, after breakfast, resuming our seats, arrived in less than three hours at Cintra. The scenery, as you approach this town, is truly enchanting. The rich and variegated wood, which clothes the side of the mountain rising above Cintra, the sunny brown, or rather the golden tinge of the mossy sward towards the crest of it, and the bare, grey, and rude-shaped rock, which crowns its lofty summit, form a picture, such as only the pencil of a master, or the pen of a poet, could attempt to sketch with fidelity. The town itself, though considerably elevated, lies far below the mountain, and all around is beauty, shade, and repose. The white and furrowed bark, and the fantastic form and growth of the pale cork tree, the low dark olive, the green leaf and golden fruit of the orange, the trellised vine, and the wild geranium, all here combine to deck the face of nature with charms, which to the eye of a northern visitor, have new and irresistible attractions. We soon left our inn, and, mounted on asses, with two sprightly boys for our guides, set forth to visit the convent, which is built nearly at the top of the Cintra mountain. You lounge at your ease, in any posture, on a large pack-saddle, covered with green cloth, and it is really surprising to see with how much safety and activity these animals carry you up paths, rocky, uneven, and dangerously steep.

A monk received us at the gate of the convent, and conducted us all over it; it is a very perfect, complete thing; but the site of it is, for singularity and boldness, unrivalled. It is secluded, utterly secluded, from the world; yet here the eye may range over the vast Atlantic, far as the strength of mortal vision permits, or may rest on lovely vales, and dark bosomed glens far beneath. The ear, too, may catch, on the one side, the hoarse voice of the rising storm; or may listen, on the other, to those pleasing and sweet sounds, which speak of rural occupations and of rural happiness.

If a man, at the age of fifty, stood alone in the world, without wife, relative, or friend, to such a spot as this might he retire for life. When death carries off our little store of affection, by laying its icy hand on the hearts where that treasure was hoarded, whither can we go for comfort? The sad bosom, and the rayless eye, are ill calculated to inspire new loves, or attract new friendships. Oh! I can imagine many cases, where the calm of a retired monastery would afford consolation to the wounded spirit. Would that cloisters were only filled with such children of misfortune!

Not very distant from this convent, on another rude eminence, stands an ancient Moorish castle, remarkable for nothing but having contained Moors. I stood on it for a quarter of an hour, and my mind's eye peopled it with its turbaned defenders. I looked out at the noble scene around me; for them, too, had the ocean smiled, and their eyes had reposed on the verdant meads, and dark groves now spread below me. There is a pleasure in

27

the association of ideas, and in the power of conjuring up, as it were, scenes and images around you, which all men have felt, but which I should labour in vain to define; from it, however, arises much of the charm of travelling. He who could stand on the solitary field of Waterloo, without imagining to himself his gallant countrymen, and their fierce opponents; or who could pass the Rubicon, without seeing the cohorts of Caesar, and their daring leader, should return to his parlour and his newspaper. In another part of this mountain, and not so lofty in its situation, is a convent, curiously built, among some wild and romantic rocks; the walls, doors, and furniture, are all of cork. Some poor humble Franciscans, inhabit it; they have a pretty garden, and a small orangery; they presented us with fruit, were very courteous, and seemed thankful for the trifle we gave them.

From hence we rode by a very agreeable path to the *Quinta* of Coulares, so highly celebrated for its delicious wine. The vale is most beautiful; in one part of it is a house, built some twenty years ago, by an English gentleman of large fortune. This mansion, surrounded as it is by every thing to make it a desirable residence, is in a state of desolation and ruin. It had been fitted up by this wealthy man in a style of the most princely magnificence; but riches cannot forbid the intrusion of sorrow, discontent, sickness, or shame. Some one of these unbidden guests drove him from this voluptuous seat, and the winds and rains of heaven, as if to mock the vain scheme of human happiness, have nearly destroyed this costly temple of pleasure.

On our return to the inn at Cintra we found a comfortable dinner, cooked and served up in the plain English fashion; well-cooled wine of Coulares, which very greatly resembles claret, left the epicure, nothing to desire; and fatigued, yet delighted with our day, we retired to excellent beds in clean, well-furnished chambers.

I rose early on the following morning, and visited the palace; it is a very ancient and curious building, and bears evident marks of having been erected on the site, and with the materials of some Moorish edifice.

All the rooms are floored with large flat tiles of a red colour, ornamented with a sort of white figuring much defaced by time. In one of the apartments you are shewn a path, worn deep by the hurried and restless footsteps of a royal captive, who was confined here for fifteen years, nearly two centuries ago. During the whole period the wretched and despicable Alphonso bore the empty and valueless title of king, while the handsome, bold, and active Pedro, his younger brother, swayed the sceptre of his realms, and revelled in the charms of her, to whom a brother had been espoused. It has been generally reported, however, by historians, that Alphonso was a prince alike impotent in body and imbecile in mind. I hope, for the sake of humanity, that such was really the case; but in countries, where civil and religious liberty is denied to the subject, truth is often strangely distorted.

We are unwilling to leave Cintra without visiting the handsome villa of the Marquis of Marialva. I was much gratified with it; it is a superb residence, every way worthy of a noble master. One chamber struck me as remarkably elegant; the walls were covered with the richest white satin, all the borders and the cornices of gold moulding, and the whole of the furniture white and gold, to correspond; there were also some fine slabs of white marble, of very extraordinary beauty.

Here, or in the adjoining chamber, the well-known convention of Cintra was signed. That it should ever have been rendered necessary, is the real, and only just cause of complaint. At the moment that it was signed, Sir Arthur Wellesley satisfactorily proved to the House of Commons, that it was a measure alike politic and expedient. I can, however, image to myself the countenance of Sir Arthur, when he saw himself arrested in the career of victory, by the arrival of a senior colleague. It has been reported, I know not with what truth, that the illustrious Wellington, after delivering his military opinion, on the field of Vimiera, from which the enemy was retiring defeated and discomfited, and after hearing the decision of Sir Harry Burrard, turned his horse's head, and with a cold and contemptuous bitterness, said aloud to his *aide-de-camp*, "You may think about dinner, for there is nothing more for soldiers to do this day."

We returned to Lisbon by Beyras, a town celebrated for having given the title of count to the great Marquis de Pombal; and where the house, and gardens, long occupied by him, are still shewn. The house merits no description; yet it was impossible to walk through the silent, and deserted chambers, without awakening the liveliest recollections of this great man's political career. Here, from this retired closet, opening on that shady terrace, perhaps this wise statesman sent forth the famous decree, which drove out the intriguing Jesuits, and banished them from Portugal. Here did he digest those plans for the general improvement of every department of the state, which, had they been promoted by, or met with less resistance from, his successors, would have given to this small kingdom, a far more honourable rank among the nations of Europe, than she has ever enjoyed. This minister's presence of mind, firmness, and activity, on that dreadful occasion when Lisbon was visited by the great earthquake, are well known. While the awful ruins of the city were yet tottering around him; while the shrieks of the wounded, the widowed, and the childless, pierced his ear; while the horrid grave of thousands was spread before him; he was seen every where encouraging and reassuring the people, calming their fears, and alleviating their distress, by all the measures which wisdom, energy, and humanity could suggest. This man, at the death of his royal master, was dismissed from office, and banished from court, and ended his days at the small village of Pombal, in the disregarded obscurity of private life.

As our carriages drove into the encampment, we were saluted by the joyful intelligence that the orders were come, and that we were to march for Spain in two days. The next day was. full of the bustle of preparation: our heavy baggage had already been left in England, and we now received a fresh order to disencumber ourselves of every thing, not absolutely necessary. My brother subaltern and I had a small baggage mule lightly laden, between us, and in this, the infancy of our zeal, we carried knapsacks; four of us formed a small social mess, and had the comfort of a canteen; but neither officers or men, at this period, had tents, and none except field officers and adjutants were mounted. One mule per company, with camp-kettles, the few baggage animals of the officers, and the train of the brigade commissariat, formed the whole of our encumbrance.

On the morning of July 28, at an early hour, we struck and delivered over our tents; three days' provision was issued to the men, and at about seven, our brigade marched from its ground, to embark for Santarem, a town about forty miles up the Tagus, whither it was arranged we were to be conveyed by water. I shall never forget my sensations on marching through the streets of Lisbon; they were filled with people; the windows crowded with faces, wearing the kindest and most animated looks; loud, long, and continued *vivas,* were poured forth on every side; shawls, handkerchiefs, and hands were waving from every balcony, and the women threw flowers and garlands on our heads. It was highly pleasing to observe this expression of public feeling on the part of the Portuguese, and I am persuaded, that, with few exceptions, the nation detested the idea of submitting to the yoke of France. That there were some of the higher classes, who, corrupted by education, blinded by fear, and unstimulated by interest or patriotism to resist the French armies, both expected their return, and wished them success, is not only probable, but certainly true. But these formed a very inconsiderable, and a very worthless part of the population. I did not form this opinion from the *vivas* of a crowd, gazing on our handsome and well-appointed troops, but from all which I had observed since I landed.

From the quay of the Commercial Square our men sprung into the boats, and our little fleet was soon sailing up the river, under a favourable breeze. It must have been a beautiful sight, for those on the quays and along the banks, to mark our fair array. The polished arms, the glittering cap-plates, and the crimson dress of the British soldiers, crowded in open barks, must have produced a very fine effect. And we, too, gazed on a scene far different indeed, but most peaceful, most lovely. The northern bank of the river from Lisbon to Villa Franca (about six leagues) presents a continued succession of rural beauties; convents, chapels, and *quintas*, gardens and vineyards, wood and verdure, cattle and groups of villagers, all blended in bright and gay confusion, arrest the eye and address the heart. Here you saw, in their cool and shaded cloisters, small parties of monks, in the dark and picturesque dress of their orders, observing us as we passed along; there some happy family, parents, children, and servants, would hurry to their garden terrace on the water's edge, and salute us with smiles and *vivas;* while a little farther, in the back ground, you might discern some solitary nun, who, from the high and grated casement of her convent, looked out upon, the strange and brilliant show, and hastily withdrew.

About two leagues above Villa Franca, the breeze died away, and not a breath of air stirred on the water. Our boatmen took to their poles, and with all their exertion, made little more than a league, when the shades of evening closed in, and we brought-to near the bank. Here we found a Portuguese tent, which had been pitched for some day-guard, but was abandoned for the night; of this my cheerful little mess took possession, and here we ate our cold meat and drank our wine, with all the gaiety of a party of pleasure.

After an hour's labour in the morning, finding we made little or no way by water, we landed and marched to Santarem. The situation of this city is very striking; it is built on bold, elevated ground, hanging directly over the Tagus, the southern bank of which it completely commands. The regiment was quartered for the night in a convent, and I received a billet on a private house. At the door of it, I was met by the owner, a gentleman-like looking well-dressed man, of about sixty, and of a very mild pleasing address: he led the way to a neat apartment, and a pretty bedchamber. I was covered with dust and dirt, and declined them as too good; but how was my confusion increased, when my host himself brought me water in a silver basin to washy while his good lady presented me with chocolate, bearing it herself on a salver. I feared that they had mistaken my rank from my two epaulettes, and I explained to them that I was a simple lieutenant. No; they well knew my rank, but did not pay me the less attention: they perfumed my chamber with rose-water, took off my knapsack with their own hands, and then left me to refresh myself by washing and dressing, and to recover from the pleasing astonishment, into which their cordial and polite reception had thrown me.

In the evening my party dined here, and the worthy host presented us with some magnums of fine old wine and the choicest fruit. We made scruples; he overruled them with true and unaffected hospitality, and we, in return, pressed on his acceptance six bottles of excellent *Sauterne*, the remains of our small stock of French wine.

Such was my treatment in the first billet I ever entered in Portugal, and such, with very few exceptions, was the character of the reception given by Portuguese of all classes, according to their means, at the commencement of the peninsula struggle, to the British army: rich and poor, the clergy and laity, the *fidalgo* and the peasant, all expressed an eagerness to serve, and a readiness to honour us. In these early marches the villa, the monastery, and the cottage were thrown open at the approach of our troops; the best apartments, the neatest cells, the humble but only beds, were all resigned to the march-worn officers. and men, with undisguised cheerfulness.

It is with pain I am compelled to confess, that the manners of my strange but well-meaning countrymen soon wrought a change in the kind dispositions of this people. When they saw many assume as a right all which they had accorded from politeness, and receive their respectful attentions, and cordial services as expressions of homage, due to the courage, wealth, and power of the British nation;—when the simplicity of their manners, their frugality, the spareness of their diet, the peculiarities of their dress, and their religious prejudices were made the subjects of derision and ridicule;—when they witnessed scenes of brutal intoxication, and were occasionally exposed to vulgar insult, from uneducated and overbearing Englishmen;—when, I say, all this occurred, they began to examine our individual titles to their esteem; they were, often, very soon disenchanted; and the spirit which we had awakened in them, manifested itself in various acts of neglect, rudeness, and even resentment.

The English are admired not only in Portugal, but over all Europe, as a free, an enlightened, and a brave people, but they cannot make themselves beloved; they are not content with being great, they must be thought so, and told so. They will not bend with good humour to the customs of other nations, nor will they condescend to soothe (flatter they never do) the harmless self-love of friendly foreigners. No: wherever they march or travel, they bear with them a haughty air of conscious superiority, and expect that their customs, habits, and opinions should supersede, or at least suspend, those of all the countries through which they pass. Among liberal-minded and well-educated Englishmen, there will ever be many bright exceptions to this general picture; and they, perhaps, will be the first to confess, that this portrait of my travelling countrymen has not been too highly coloured.

CHAPTER 3

Into Spain

Santarem, like all other cities in Portugal, has its convents, churches, and chapels, the natural pride of its citizens, and the objects which all idlers and strangers visit. There is little remarkable in any of them. At their university I passed half an hour in conversation with one of the professors. He requested me to read for him a page of Virgil, after the manner of my country. I did so; and returning the book to him, he also read one: no third person could have supposed, that we had been reading the same language. Our pronunciation may, and from habit does undoubtedly sound the richest to an English ear; but theirs is certainly the nearest to the Italian, and perhaps, therefore to the Roman. There are not very many students at this college, and as they are almost all educated for the church or the cloister, their studies are entirely confined to theology, and their reading to the perusal of sacred biography, such as the lives of the saints, martyrs, and holy men. As the shades of evening closed in, our column formed in the plain below the town, and commenced its march to Golegâo, a large village about four leagues distant

With a small advanced guard I entered Golegâo at the head of the regiment, just as early *matin*-bell was summoning the inhabitants to prayer. The attendance on public worship throughout Spain and Portugal is extremely regular, and no occupation, or manner of life, is suffered to interfere with this sacred duty. To mass go the muleteers before they load their train; and from the door of the chapel the peasants sally forth to their daily labours.

The very changing of night into day, a measure rendered necessary by the extreme heat, carried with it the charm of novelty. I was well lodged, and hospitably treated, in a humble but clean cottage, and with the night again set forward.

This march, and the following, our route, which passed by Punhete to Abrantes, led us often for miles along the banks of the Tagus, and through villages built on the very edge of the river. A clear bright silver moon lighted our silent path; not a lamp burning in any of the cottages; not a human voice to be heard: not a sound, save the dull tread of our weary men, and the gentle tone in which the waters told their ceaseless flow. The moon-beams which played upon the bright arms of our gallant soldiers, shone also on the glistening nets of the peaceful fishermen, which hung spread upon the rocks near his deserted bark. All within these humble dwellings was repose, and their happy inmates slumbered sweetly unconscious that the tide of war (harmless and friendly indeed to them, yet bearing on its wave not only youth, ambition, and courage, but, perhaps, even ferocity and crime,) foiled, in the dead of night, past the vine-clad walls of their defenceless cots. The town of Abrantes is well situated; it stands lofty, and commands the passage of the Tagus, over which, this point, a bridge of boats communicates with the southern provinces. We crossed the river, and occupied for one night a camp of standing huts, formed many weeks before by. some division of our army, which had halted in that neighbourhood. At sunrise the following morning we were again in motion, and marched onwards to the village of Gaviao. Our road led, in part, through plains coveted with gumcistus in flower, the frail leaves of which are remarkable for their delicate whiteness; and in part, over uplands all clothed with heath, but a heath so rich in the variety, the beauty, and the fragrance of its plants, that the traveller forgot, or forgave, the absence of the corn-field, the vineyard, and the cottage.

As the chill, dews of evening were descending on our bivouack, near this last village, a staff-officer, with a courier, cattle galloping into it, and alighted at the quarter of our general. It was soon known among us, that a severe and sanguinary action had been fought by our brother soldiers at Talavera. Disjointed rumours spoke of a dear-bought field, a heavy loss, and a subsequent retreat I well remember how we all gathered round our fires to listen, to conjecture, and to talk about this glorious, but bloody, event. We all naturally regretted that, in the honours of such a day, we had borne no share; and talked long, and with an undefined pleasure, about the carnage. Yes, strange as it may appear, soldiers, and not they alone, talk of the slaughter of battle-fields with a sensation, which, though it suspends the lively throb of the gay and careless heart, partakes, nevertheless, of pleasure. Nay, I will go farther; in the very exposure of the person to the peril of sudden and violent death, cureless wounds, and ghastly laceration, excitement, strong, high, and pleasurable, fills and animates the bosom: hope, pride, patriotism, and awe, make up this mighty feeling, and lift a man, for such moments, almost above the dignity of his nature. Such moments are more than equal to years of common life. And where, on the 28th of July, when death was gathering her bleeding victims in the field of Talavera, where then were we?—That very day we were sailing on the Tagus' ample bosom: our eyes resting on scenes of smiling peace and romantic loveliness, and our hearts beating high and hopefully.

Our drum beat two hours before the dawn of day, and at an early hour we reached Niza; not, however, before the sun had acquired such fierce and burning power, as to strike me down thrice, in a very few minutes. During a short halt, I threw myself on the parched-up grass, and sleep overcame me; my hat fell off, and the scorching rays of the sun shone full upon my naked head: awaked by the sound of the bugle, I suddenly rose, but immediately fell senseless; my brother officers recovered me by the usual means, but on my attempting to stand, the same violent effect was twice more produced.

Three days' rest at Niza quite restored me, and I was enabled to resume all my duties. During this short interval the troops had, luckily for me, halted. On the fourth morning we marched to cross the Tagus at Villa Velha, and pursued our route to Zarzala Major, the first town on the Spanish frontier, in the road to Placentia. This movement was made, I believe, without any instruction from Sir Arthur Wellesley; and had for its object the diversion of Soult's force, which was known to have arrived in the neighbourhood of Coria and Placentia; and which, it was thought, might act offensively against the British, on their retreat from Talavera; which, encumbered as they were with wounded, could not have immediately followed the battle, or been effected with any extraordinary rapidity.

The scenery on this march, after passing the Tagus, is not very remarkable; but the road from Niza to Villa Velha is truly romantic; and the river, at that point, forcing its narrow, deep, and angry course between lofty and precipitous banks, which rise into brown and barren mountains, forms a grand and imposing picture. We bivouacked daily. It is a pleasing sight to see a column arrive at its halting ground. The camp is generally marked out, if circumstances allow of it, on the edge of some wood, and near a river or stream. The troops are halted in open columns, arms piled, picquets and guards paraded and posted, and, in two minutes, all appear at home. Some fetch large stones to form fire-places; others hurry off with canteens and kettles for water, while the wood resounds with the blows of the bill-hook.

Dispersed, under the more distant trees, you see the officers: some dressing; some arranging a few bought to shelter them by night; others kindling their own fires; while the most active are seen returning from the village, laden with bread, or, from some flock of goats, feeding near us, with a supply of new milk. How often, under some spreading cork-tree, which offered shade, shelter, and fuel, have I taken up my lodging for the night; and here, or by some gurgling stream, my bosom fanned by whatever air was stirring, made my careless toilet, and sat down with men I both liked and esteemed, to a coarse but wholesome meal, seasoned by hunger and by cheerfulness. The rude simplicity of this life I found most pleasing. An enthusiastic admirer of nature, I was glad to move and dwell amid her grandest scenes, remote from cities, and unconnected with what is called society. Her mountains, her forests, and, sometimes, her bare and blade-less plains, yielding me a passing home: her rivers, streams, and springs, cooled my brow, and allayed my thirst. The inconvenience of one camp taught me to enjoy the next; and I learned. (a strange lesson for the thoughtless) that wood and water, shade and grass, were luxuries. I saw the sun set every evening: I saw him rise again each morning in all his majesty, and I felt that my very existence was a blessing. Strange, indeed, to observe how soon men, delicately brought up, can inure themselves to any thing. Wrapt in a blanket, or a cloak, the head reclining on a stone or a knapsack, covered by the dews of night, or drenched perhaps by the thunder-shower, sleeps many a youth, to whom the carpeted chamber, the curtained couch, and the bed of down, have been from infancy familiar.

As we forded the river Elga, which, on the road we were marching, divides Portugal and Spain, I promised myself much pleasure from seeing a town inhabited by Spaniards, whose language, manners, customs, and dress, I knew, differed widely from the Portuguese, and were, from national pride, kept quite as distinct on the frontiers as elsewhere. Our column passed close to the town of Zarza, and took up its ground on a bare, rocky eminence, about a mile in front. Not a soul came out to meet us, not a soul followed us to our bivouack. All was still as at midnight, yet the noon-day sun shone fiercely down.

No sooner was my regiment dismissed, than I hastened into the town, and entered it among the first. The streets were deserted, and the houses barred; the church alone stood open, but the plate from the altar and the contents of the sacristy, had been removed. The market-place indeed was fast filling with our Spanish muleteers, and, from their dress and language, you might almost have fancied them inhabitants: but you looked around in vain for women and children to favour this illusion; the sound of their soft and innocent voices was nowhere to be heard, and in the unmoved features of our muleteers, you could not trace the anxious feelings of the husband and the father.

I passed out of the town by a narrow lane, which led towards some gardens; as I walked slowly on, full of thought, my eye was attracted by the sight of a pair of castanets, which, dropped in the hurry of flight, lay directly in the path: to how much of innocent delight, youthful pleasure, and parental pride, had these little symbols of happier and more tranquil times been witnesses!—Oh! England—thou enviable spot—thou "precious stone set in the silver sea," from how many of the evils of war do thy rocks and waves protect thee!—I turned aside into a garden, and saw a peasant at the further end of it, who, on perceiving me, fled, and would have concealed himself: I overtook him, and reassuring him by my voice and manner, he became communicative. From him I learnt, that the inhabitants of Zarza had expected the French that morning, and, dreading their arrival, had all fled in the course of the night, some to Alcantara, others to the woods and mountains, I purchased some very fine musk and water-melons from this peasant, paying him a trifle more than their value, which appeared to excite very strongly both his astonishment and gratitude.

The scene of this morning made a deep and lasting impression on me. It is true that I have since witnessed horrors, which might well have taught me to think lightly of an occurrence, which I afterwards found was not uncommon; but first impressions are too powerful to be ever forgotten. The greater part of this day, too, the thermometer had been from ninety-five to ninety-eight, another reason for remembering Zarza and the scorching unsheltered bivouack.

CHAPTER 4

Spain, Spaniards & Soldiers

The next morning our general returned from a conference with Marshal Beresford, who was in the neighbourhood of Pena Garcia and Pena Macor, with a body of Portuguese, and the same evening we retreated across the Elga and re-entered Portugal; a movement rendered prudent, I believe, by the force and vicinity of the enemy, for we had only six battalions, unsupported by cavalry or artillery. We now retraced our steps to Alemtejo. One of our camps, on this short retreat, was formed on ground the most wild and picturesque. Halfway between Villa Velha and Niza, the road winds through a deep and narrow valley, inclosed on all sides by rudely-shaped and rocky hills; through it flows a small streamlet, descending from the heights in the rugged channel of a wintry torrent, and faintly marking out its course with a silvery thread of the purest water.

Here, at nightfall, after being nearly eighteen hours under arms, we halted: the heights ascend on all sides of this little vale so steep and perpendicular, that it is impossible to preserve any regular formation, and the men were dispersed in groups all up the hills. I and my companions spread our cloaks and kindled our fire upon a rocky ledge, close to the top of that ravine down which the rivulet fell, and thus we overlooked the whole encampment. The short dry brushwood, though it made bad fires, sent forth bright and beauteous. flames, and the sudden and magic illumination of this rude and warlike scene may be conceived, but, I feel, it is impossible to describe it. The fitful glare which gave to view the groups of soldiers, here only showing the dark outlines of human figures, and there throwing a fiery light on their arms, their dress, and features, the glow reflected from the stream, and the dark, lofty masses of hill and rock in the back ground, formed a picture such as only the genius of a Byron, or a Southey, could convey to the mind of a reader in the language of description.

We halted at Niza for a fortnight, and hutted in a wood near the town. Here, in a thick well-built bower, with a bed of heath, a large smooth slate, to serve for a table, and a bench of cork, I lived as comfortably, and, from the novelty, far more contentedly, than I should have done in the best-furnished apartments in England.

On the 7th of September, we broke up from Niza, and marched into cantonments in Spanish Estremadura. Our route passed by Portalegre, Elvas, Badajos, and Talavera Real. The valley by which you approach Portalegre, is fertile and very beautiful. *quintas,* gardens, vineyards, and corn-fields, cover the last six miles on your road to the city, which is airy, well-built, and handsomely situated on a lofty eminence, sheltered to the north by mountains, planted with vines to their very summits, and overlooked on the south by heights, richly clothed with wood to the very edge of the grey and broken ridges of rock which crown them. To the eastward it commands a fine and boundless prospect over the undulating plains, which stretch in the direction of Badajos and Elvas.

We were billeted for the night in this city, and, after dressing in a cool, retired apartment, which opened into a small orangery, I visited the cathedral: it is handsome, has a fine-toned organ, and the singing was sweet. It was the evening service, and afterwards I heard a requiem chaunted or sung over the grave of some deceased person of rank; there was a long procession, and several monks assisted, all bearing torches; surrounding the graven stone, under which lay the mouldering remains of this wealthy corpse, or rather once wealthy man, they broke forth into a fine and solemn strain. The number of deep and powerful bass voices, contrasted with the soft and feminine tones of the youthful choristers, produced a very grand; effect, far superior to anything ever heard in our cathedral service, I am free, however, to confess, that the singing of some individuals in our English choirs, is not easily to be surpassed; still, we never hear that astonishing bass which peals forth from a large assemblage of priests and friars, and which is, at once, so awful and so truly imposing.

The light brigade, under General Robert Crawford, was quartered in Portalegre at this time. The regiments composing it were very fine, and in the highest possible order they had had the mortification of joining Lord Wellington's army on the field of Talavera, the day after the battle. I here saw the parade of the 95th Regiment, a corps as generally, as it is justly, admired. We continued our march the next day, halting at Arronches, a small, unimportant town, and from thence proceeded the following morning to a bivouack under the walls of Elvas. Near this last town two men in the column died on the line of march, from the joint effects of heat and fatigue. The thermometer rose, in the course of that day, to 100 in the open air.

Elvas is a frontier town of strength, and boasts the protection of an impregnable out-fort (La Lippe), which is looked upon as a *chef-d'oeuvre* of skill in the art of fortification. The hospitals of our army were established in this town; and, in walking through the streets, or passing the convents appropriated to them, my eyes continually rested on men, who had been wounded in the late battle of Talavera. As I returned the salutes of these gallant sufferers, I felt my cheek glow like scarlet. What would I not then have given, for the proud privilege of being numbered with those officers, who had commanded them in the field of honour, and who now, their contracted limbs supported by crutches, or their shattered arms lightly suspended in black silk handkerchiefs, were moving indolently in the cool shade, with that contented look, which the sensation of returning health always bestows, and here doubly interesting from a consciousness of the noble cause, which had stretched them on

43

the bed of pain. I followed a large group of them into the shop of a Moorish sutler, called Tamet, well known to all the British army as the Turk.

This man sold almost every thing which could be useful to officers on service, and was civil and liberal, far more so than any one in his situation, I ever met with. Here, while making a few purchases, I listened eagerly to the conversation around me. It was of a character to me deeply interesting; for they spoke of our political relations with Spain, of the military character of the Spaniards, and of the prospects of the war; but I confess I quite blushed for their want of information and liberality. The contempt with which they spoke of Spanish prowess, was not only uncharitable, but unmerited; the generous and fearless ardour with which the Spaniards first rushed to arms, and intrepidly threw down the gauntlet of defiance to that man, before whom Italy, Austria, Prussia, and Russia had successively bent the knee, and yielded up the palm of victory; the heroic perseverance with which they endured toil, privation, and defeat; the undying resolution with which, though daily routed they still presented themselves before the victorious legions of a brave and skilful enemy, and retired from one field, only to offer themselves as willing victims on another: the unexampled heroism with which Zaragoza, and some other towns, were defended by their inhabitants, without distinction of age or sex; all these were facts, which ought to have been known to my fellow-countrymen, and on the memory of which the impartial soldier, and the good man, will ever dwell with enthusiasm and delight—I had evidently been unfortunate in the group; for, I believe, that in no army of Europe are so many gentlemen, and men of education and independent feeling to be found, as in our own.

But, the British army must not be made responsible for the folly and ignorance of many, who have been too much honoured by admission into her ranks. We must not look to all who have fought our battles, in the vain hope of meeting heroes; we shall find but men.—No.—Scars and decorations can only effectually ennoble men of virtue, of sense, and of courage—If, however, the romantic illusions of a youthful and heated fancy have been destroyed by observation and inquiry, my attachment to the profession of arms has not deserted me; confirmed and happy in my choice of it, I now follow it with more silent devotion, more rational hopes, and less obtrusive zeal. I passed the evening of this day under a canopy of luxuriant and shady vines, which stretched their creeping stems over the trellis-work of a covered garden-path. Here, by the side of a well, our humble repast was spread; the green and purple clusters hanging over our heads, afforded us an excellent dessert; and, after drinking some fine well-cooled wine of Borba, I rolled myself in my cloak and slept soundly, till, roused by drums and bugles, I sprung up, and hastened to fall in with the column, which was on this day to enter Spain.

After descending from Elvas, the road to Badajos lies over a brown and level plain, which, extending far beyond that city, seems only bounded by the horizon; though here and there in the distance, a few blue mountains may be seen; but these only rise like rocky islands in the ocean, and serve rather to mark more strongly the dreary flatness, than to vary that fatiguing prospect, or relieve the aching sight.

A shallow and nameless rivulet marks the confines of Portugal, and, passing this strange limit, you enter the kingdom of Spain. A few miles beyond this, you traverse the city of Badajos, in front of which we bivouacked for the night. The town of Badajos is fortified, and though it certainly did not present the appearance of great strength, its defences were afterwards so much improved by the French, while they held it, as to cost us in the reduction of it, in 1812, a very heavy and murderous loss. Many a man smiled in those days at the insignificant appearance of its works, who was doomed to perish in the assault, which restored it to our arms. It is in the market place, and the streets of Badajos, that the stranger soon discovers that he is among another people, and in a separate, and, were it not for the dust of Portugal still covering his dress, he might almost judge, in a remote kingdom.

A chain of mountains, or a spacious channel, could hardly prepare him for a greater change. Features, carriage, costume, language, and manners, all proclaim a distinct race. The style of building, too, differs: fewer windows front the streets, and most of these are grated with long bars, curving outwards at the bottom. The larger houses have a small square court within, ornamented with a fountain, and embellished with plants in large pots, or frames of wood; round this court the building runs, putting forth a covered balcony, into which the windows of the residence look. The countenance of the Spaniard is noble, his stature tall, his walk erect, his deportment haughty: his manner of speaking varies greatly; it is generally grave and solemn, but on points of deep interest and feeling, is animated beyond expression. There is very great variety in the costume of Spaniards, for the natives of each province are readily distinguished by their dress, and, when you see an assemblage of men from various parts of Spain, the effect is very striking. The market-place of Badajos, which, at the time I saw it, was crowded with strangers, had all the appearance of a picturesque and well-arranged masquerade. The different modes of dress, ancient, and not liable to daily changes, are, no doubt, the same they were four centuries ago.

The Estremaduran himself has a brown jacket without a collar, and with sleeves, which lace at the shoulder, so that they we removed at pleasure. The red sash is universally worn, and a cloak is generally carried on the left arm. A jacket and waistcoat profusely ornamented with silk lace, and buttons of silver filigree, the hair clubbed, and tied with broad black ribbon, and a neat cap of cloth, or velvet, mark the Andalusian. The ass-driver of Cordova, is clothed in a complete dress of the tawny brown leather of his native province.

The lemonade seller of Valencia has a linen shirt open at the neck, a fancy waistcoat without sleeves, a kilt of white cotton, white stockings rising to the calf, and sandals. Muleteers, with their broad body-belts of buff leather, their *capitans* or train masters, with the ancient cartridge-belts, and the old Spanish gun, were mingled in these groups. Here, too, were many officers and soldiers of the patriot armies, which, raised in haste, were not regularly or uniformly clothed, if I except some of the old standing force. Of these, you might see the royal *carabineer*, with the cocked hat, blue coat faced with red, and, instead of boots, the ancient greaves, of thick hard black leather, laced at the sides. The dragoon, in a uniform of yellow, black belts, and a helmet with a crown of brass. The royal, or Walloon guards, in their neat dress of blue and red, with white lace: the common soldier in brown. Mingled with these was the light-horseman, in a hussar jacket of brown, and overalls capped, lined, and vandyked at the bottom with tan leather; here, again, a peasant with the cap and coat of a soldier, there, a soldier from Navarre, or Arragon, with the bare foot, and the light hempen sandal of his country.

There was a pleasure I took in the contemplation of these scenes, which the deep interest I felt in the fate of the unfortunate Spaniards, very greatly enhanced. They are people of the most primitive, and uncorrupted singleness of heart; a people, whose national character is very ill understood, and has been very often, and very cruelly misrepresented. Shut out from; the rest of Europe by their geographical position, having long since ceased to be a commercial people, and their country, grand and beautiful as are its features, being little visited, from its utter want of convenience and accommodation for travellers, the Spaniards, until the late contest, had been long lost, sight of. The rays of science and of truth, which had enlightened other nations, shone not on wretched Spain; the institutions for civil and religious liberty, which had given new dignity and value to existence, over half, Europe, were there unknown, and the Spaniards themselves trembled at the march of improvement, which they heard only, as of a spirit of destruction, from whose wrathful, though salutary visitations, they were happy to be spared. Such apathy was appalling, but it was not incurable; their energies lay dormant, but were not dead. Enervated, by the conquest of America, a conquest achieved by such high and heroic enterprise, as gives to historical detail all the charm and the splendour of romance, but which opened on them the floodgates of wealth, and its attendant miseries, the Spaniards neglected to promote domestic trade, manufactures, and husbandry. They had been a martial people; such are usually averse to daily labour and habitual exertion: the countries of Europe, however, had by successful leagues shaken their power, and circumscribed their means of indulging this restless passion for glory. Their swords might then have been turned into ploughshares, and they might have become peacefully industrious and prosperously happy. They were made, however, by the easy conquest of New Spain, suddenly, and without effort, wealthy, and from this misfortune they have never yet recovered.

Let us briefly examine the common charges now preferred against them. They are accused of being indolent, and it is true that they are not very laborious, for their wants are few, and these by the fruitfulness of their soil are readily supplied; but they are not half so indolent as prejudiced travellers would pretend. It is objected, that, in many of their provinces, there are spacious tracts of land uncultivated. On enquiry you will find, that there is no water to assist in fertilizing many of these deserts, while others have been set apart as public sheep walks, by the authority of the government, for whose impolicy in sanctioning so absurd a custom, the wretched and powerless inhabitants must not be condemned. If, however, an appearance of cultivation is the true criterion of industry, in many of their mountainous districts, well supplied with water, we see vines and fruit trees on the steepest cliffs, and corn produced in small plots of ground, on the summits of precipitous and rocky mountains, inaccessible save to the active goat, and the laborious peasant.

The Spaniards are often despised for their ignorance. It is true, that, in the philosophy of nature and metaphysical inquiry, they are far behind most other nations in Europe; but, in such principles of moral ethics, as should regulate human conduct, they are well versed, and their practice keeps pace with their knowledge. On such subjects they have a dignified and forceful eloquence, which would confound the mere scholar. Unpractised in schools, and little acquainted with books, experience, and observation form them, and they can boast of solid characters, and sound judgements.

The Spaniards are reproached with being very superstitious; and they are so. But superstition is not always the parent of crime. Those who would attribute to a willing and consenting nation, the establishment of that merciless tribunal, the Inquisition, greatly err; that barbarous institution originated in the wicked and detestable policy of cruel rulers and crafty ecclesiastics, who built up their iniquitous power upon the piety, reverence, and zeal of a devout and enthusiastic people.

The Spaniards, blessed with a fertile imagination and a lively fancy, are exalted, consoled, or awed, by the strange creations and idols of their subject minds. The arm is nerved with tenfold: vigour, the heart steeled with tenfold courage, the tear of affliction is dried, or the commission of crime averted by feelings of irresistible influence, the offspring of holy superstition. In a country where the laws are ill administered, this authority of conscience rules the heart of each individual, and with such success, that I do not hesitate to say, I think there are fewer atrocious crimes committed in Spain, than in the British islands: there is more manslaughter, but less murder, less deliberate assassination.

There are bands of robbers in their mountain-passes, and their extensive forests, but, there are fewer villains in their towns and villages, and crimes are rarely heard of in the peaceful bosom of their inoffensive societies. The Spaniards are hospitable and generous, and unaffectedly so: they are good fathers, and husbands, humane, and considerate masters of families. They are patriotic and brave, temperate and honest. I am here speaking of the mass of the Spanish people, of her citizens, her yeomen, and her peasantry, not of the nobler and more wealthy classes; for among these, alas! many examples of degeneracy are to be found. Some of these have lost all, which made the Spaniard respectable, without acquiring that which has given the more polished and enlightened inhabitants of other countries their admitted superiority. For myself, I look forward eagerly to that moment, when forced, by the loss of her American colonies, to examine her resources at home, and to learn the true value of her possessions in the Peninsula, Spain shall, once more, exhibit herself in greatness and in glory to astonished Europe;—when she will forget her ancient maxim, that it is wiser to bear with the failings of kings, than to punish them;—when she will have firmness enough to represent her grievances, and resolution enough to insist on their redress;—when she will abolish the impious and hellish powers of the Inquisition, and secure to herself liberty without licentiousness, and religion without persecution.

These observations may seem perhaps misplaced. It may be so: but I do not follow the order either of a traveller or narrator. My travels and campaigns are over, and I am rather mingling past and present reflections, than confining myself to the ordinary detail of first sights and first impressions.

I wandered about the town for some hours, and walked in the evening on their *alameda*, or promenade. Here I saw several fine and beautiful women. The dress of the Spanish lady is remarkably elegant, and generally adorns a very perfect shape. Black is the universal colour, and the robe is most tastefully worked and vandyked. A *mantilla*, or veil of black silk or lace, and sometimes of white lace, is thrown over the head, and, leaving the face uncovered, falls gracefully over the shoulders, and is confined at the waist by the arms of the wearer. They are both expensive and particular in dressing their feet with neatness, and their little shoes fit closely. The large black eye, the dark expressive glance, the soft blood-tinged olive of the glowing complexion, make the unwilling Englishman confess the majesty of Spanish beauty, and, he feels that though the soft blue eye, and delicate loveliness of his own countrywomen awaken more tender feelings of interest, he would deny, or dispute in vain, the commanding superiority of these dark-eyed and fine-formed damsels.

The gentlemen and noblemen who walked with them had nothing striking in their appearance: the cocked hat was universally worn, and their dress in other respects, resembled that which the French wore some thirty years ago. I turned with much satisfaction to a group of English officers then passing, who were all fine-looking young men; and I observed several Spaniards of the middling and lower classes (the true and proper samples of that people), drawing comparisons between them and their own degenerate *hidalgos*, very greatly to the advantage of my countrymen.

I left the town highly gratified with all I had seen and heard, yet somewhat disappointed that I had not, with all my watching and loitering near his quarters, succeeded in catching one glance at Wellington, whom at that time, I had never seen. My comrades had again found a garden near the bivouack; and after a very delightful evening I lay down on a mat, spread for me by one of the gardeners, without even a cloak, and composed myself to sleep. Such is the climate of Spain.

We reached Torre Major, the village allotted to our brigade, in two days, passing through and bivouacking for the night near Talavera. Some regiments of the division Hill, to which our brigade was attached, lay at Montijo, a town in our route, about four miles from Torre Major; among others the Twenty-Ninth Regiment. It was the first corps distinguished for its services, which I had ever seen under arms. Nothing could possibly be worse than their clothing; it had become necessary to patch it; and as red cloth could not be procured, grey, white, and even brown had been used: yet, under this striking disadvantage, they could not be viewed by a soldier without admiration. The perfect order and cleanliness of their arms and appointments, their steadiness on parade, their erect carriage, and their firm and free marching, exceeded any thing of the kind which I had ever seen. No corps of any army, or nation, which I have since had an opportunity of seeing, has come nearer to my idea of what a regiment of infantry should be, than the old Twenty-Ninth.

Our village was a collection of mud cottages, not a tree near it, and looked, as we approached, poor and mean: we were, however, very agreeably surprised on entering it. The dwelling of the Spanish peasant is very clean, and owing to the extreme thickness of the walls, and the smallness of the windows, delightfully cool.

I got a comfortable little room, with a good bed, two or three of the little low chairs, and the small low table of the country. The poorer Spaniards sit very low, and their food is spread on a table still lower, a custom very ancient and very inconvenient I however thought myself in high luck to be lord of this little sanctum, and generally retired to rest too much fatigued to find fault with my thick hard mattress, and my coarse though white sheets.

The life of the Spanish villager is simple, and not without its pleasures. He rises early, and after mass goes forth to labour: a bit of dry bread and a few grapes, or a slice of the water-melon, supply his breakfast: a plain dish of vegetables, generally a sort of bean, boiled with the smallest morsel of bacon to flavour it, forms the dinner; and their drink is water, or the weak common wine of the country. They invariably, whether in their houses or in the fields, take their *siesta* after dinner, and proceed again to labour in the cool of the evening. In the front of their cottages you may almost always see low benches of stone: on these, after supper, they seat themselves to smoke their *segars*; and here, surrounded by their families, they frequently remain till a late hour, enjoying the refreshing air of night, and all the luxury of that calm and lovely season, so grateful and reviving in their warm climate.

How often have I stood apart and gazed on these happy groups, how often have I listened to their pleasing ditties, the pauses and cadences of which they mark so feelingly, yet so simply, with the light guitar!

Oftentimes too, when the moon shines brightly, their youth will meet together, and by that soft light, dance to the cheerful sound of the merry castanets, the rude but sprightly *fandango*, or the more graceful *bolero* of their country. What is there to despise or ridicule in a life like this? Yet I have often met among my countrymen, with those who would laugh with contempt at the innocent, and not irrational, amusements of this contented peasantry.

Some of their customs in husbandry are very ancient, among others, the treading out of their corn with cattle, instead of threshing it. This is all done in the open air, where the grain is afterwards spread to dry and harden; oxen or mares are used for this purpose, and you may see five or six at a time trotting round in a circle, upon the out-spread wheat in straw. This practice obtained in the very earliest ages of the world, and one cannot therefore look upon it, without awakening in the mind, by the natural laws of suggestion, a train of the most interesting recollections.

I made an excursion from our cantonment in this village to the town of Merida, a place of some note, situated on the Guadiana, about four leagues in front of us. Myself, a friend, and an acquaintance from another corps, who has long since been numbered with the slain, set off at an early hour, and after a pleasant ride of two hours, reached Merida. We procured a billet for the day, as a place of retreat, and immediately after breakfast, though the midday heat was scorching and oppressive; walked forth to see those monuments of antiquity for which Merida is so deservedly celebrated among well-informed Spaniards, but of which I never even heard or read, till accidentally cantoned in Estremadura. This city was founded by Augustus, and the lands around it were granted by him to the veterans of some disbanded cohorts, who had long and faithfully served the empire.

On entering Merida, you pass the Guadiana by a handsome stone bridge[3] of Roman architecture, and in the highest state of preservation; above it, on ground the most elevated in the city, stands a Roman castle[4], the venerable walls of which, though rough and discoloured, or rather, coloured by the touch of time, appear secure and undecayed. These antiquities of themselves would have well rewarded our visit, for the design of them had probably been given by some celebrated Roman architect eighteen centuries before; and conquered Spaniards, from whose hands the shield and the sword so long, but so vainly, opposed to their invaders, had been reluctantly dropped, were

---

3. This bridge has sixty-four arches, and is one thousand yards in length; the antiquary will learn with sorrow, that two arches of this old bridge were, in the spring of 1812, blown up by the British, in the course of their military operations in the province of Estremadura.
4. This castle was of great extent, the centre area being two hundred yards square.

employed, perhaps, in raising these monuments of the greatness, the power, and the genius of their victors. Such was the policy of the Romans: they always thus, by the erection of public works of magnificence and utility, while they recorded their own triumphs, gilt over the very chains they imposed, and made their provincial subjects feel proud even of dependency. Merida had its amphitheatre, its *naumachia*, its baths, its triumphal arches, its temples and votive altars.

In a plain near the city are very grand and striking remains of the amphitheatre.[5] Its form, except in height, is still preserved; the seats appear quite perfect; the vaulted dens where the beasts were confined, and which open on the arena, are uninjured, and their arched roofs are strong as ever; the whole building is of stone, and the Roman cement used in its construction, is as hard, and seems to have been as durable, as the stone itself. Not very distant, you distinctly trace the *naumachia*[6]; and the low stone channel or conductor, by which the hollow space or basin was filled with water, may still be seen. Crowded on the seats of this amphitheatre, or pressing round the sides of the *naumachia*, you may still fancy the haughty legionaries, and the wondering Spaniards, gazing on the magnificent exhibitions of those splendid ages.

As you pass from this scene towards the town, you are struck by the lofty and picturesque ruins of two aqueducts[7], one erected by the Romans, the other built by the Moors. I defy any man, of common education and feeling, to look upon such memorials of other days, unmoved.

I wandered from my companions, and seating myself under the shade of the first, fell into a train of thought, at once solemn and delightful. Here, on this very spot, had the Roman eagle

---

5. This amphitheatre has two tiers of seats, seven rows in the lower, five in the upper. Its diameter is fifty paces, and it is capable of holding with ease more than two thousand spectators.

6. The basin of this *naumachia* is one hundred paces by sixty, its form oval, its depth twenty feet in the centre, and the banks for the spectators rise about twenty feet above its sides.

7. The Roman aqueduct has three tiers of arches, the Moorish only two.

been displayed in the day of its pride and glory; here, Roman knights and soldiers, men horn perhaps on the banks of the Tiber, and educated in imperial Rome, whose familiar language was that in which a Cicero wrote, and a Virgil sung, and who had served and fought in Greece and Asia, laid down their helm and *cuirass*, and claimed their hardly-earned reward.

Over the same plain had the rude and unlettered Goths moved as conquerors, till in turn the haughty and glittering crescent rose o'er their drooping banner, and countless Moors, known by their snowy turbans, and silken vests, borne on the fleet coursers of Africa, and brandishing their curved *falchions* in all the insolence of triumph, rode shouting to those walls which an Augustus had built, and over which a Trajan had once held sway.

There is something infinitely affecting in having such scenes forced upon our imaginations by the presence of monuments, which, though crumbling before the ceaseless and consuming power of time, have yet survived, for so many centuries, the perishable hands of the mortals who raised them. There is a pleasure too, though it is not perhaps a Christian one: we are gratified, when reflecting on the shortness, uncertainty, and obscurity of our own lives, to mark the silent triumph of time, alike "o'er all that has been, o'er all that is;" for the very wrecks of antiquity, still scattered over the earth, serve but to proclaim, more sadly, the desolating and enduring tyranny of time. In one of the streets of Merida may be seen a large and lofty arch[8], said to be a triumphal one, erected in honour of Trajan. It bears, however, no inscription, nor is it in any way adorned with sculpture or relief; it has, nevertheless, the true Roman character; it is handsome in its proportions, and solid in its construction: very large massive stones, arranged with the most just and admirable skill, and put together without cement, compose this still perfect work.

In another part of the city three votive altars have been raised one above the other, and form a sort of pillar, on the top of which, some good and devout fathers have very provokingly placed the

---

8. This arch is fifty feet in height, and the base and sides of it are exceedingly thick.

clumsy image of a saint. Strange revolution! that altars sculptured and adorned by the hands of heathens and idolaters, should now form a column to elevate a statue for Christian adoration.

Near this place two small chapels have been built out of the materials, and upon the sites, of Roman temples; one of these, now dedicated to the Virgin, has the following inscription in large Roman characters, immediately above the entrance: "*Marti Sacrum.*"

The baths are surprisingly perfect, but not large, though they have evidently been very handsome. You descend to them by a long flight of stone steps; the subterraneous chambers are gloomy, and riot spacious, but extremely cool; the basins still contain water, supplied by some spring, but they are foul from neglect and disuse. These bathing rooms are lighted from the top of the building, which just above the water is open; a cornice runs round these rooms, most curiously and delicately finished, and the vine leaves and bunches of grapes, thus represented, appear as perfect as if they had not been executed many years. There are, doubtless, more vestiges of Roman sculpture and masonry scattered and lost in the materials with which several of the private houses in and about Merida have been erected; and the foundation of many an old building, and the bed of many a garden, would well reward the search and labour of an antiquary. The remains which I have noticed, are all that the eager traveller can now discover; they are, however, sufficient in number, and interesting enough in character, to throw a sacred and indescribable charm around this small but venerable city.

CHAPTER 5

The Kindness of Strangers

In our billet, whither we returned to dinner, we found our *patrona* not a little fidgety and anxious at the idea of our having passed the hottest hours of the day exposed to the burning rays of the sun; the Spaniards themselves are very cautious in this particular, and usually shut up their windows, and confine themselves to their houses, if not to their beds, during the oppressive heat of noon. This good lady was civil and full of conversation: she had two daughters, one of whom, the youngest, a girl of about seventeen, was without any exception, the most lovely, the most beautiful woman I saw while in Spain. To a very perfect form, she added a most faultless and most expressive countenance: never shall I forget her graceful, elegant movements, and the natural, yet chastened animation with which she spoke. I have never seen her since the moment that we mounted our horses to return; she leaned gracefully over the balcony, and kissed her hand to us as we rode off, wishing us success and honour in war, with all that noble enthusiasm which stamps the Spanish heroine. In the course of our conversation, she had expressed herself warmly about the profession of arms, saying repeatedly, that she would accept the hand of no man who had not fought for his country, and who was not a true Spaniard. Was Spain a country to be subdued, when such was the spirit of her daughters?

As we passed out of the town, we saw several officers, men, and horses of the heavy brigade of British cavalry, stationed there. The cattle were in wretched condition, and the men looked sickly. Both officers and privates were very ill dressed, and their brown and shapeless hats had a most unmilitary appearance. Whoever had seen these, regiments in England; in pale, sallow-looking men, and skeleton horses, would hardly have recognized the Third Dragoon Guards and Fourth Dragoons, two corps enjoying, and deservedly, a well-earned name. Thus, oftentimes, on actual service, vanishes all that brilliancy which has won the heart and fixed the choice of so many a youth, and which appeared so gay and attractive on crowded esplanades at home.

We pursued our way, for a few miles, slowly and silently, for we had too much food for reflection to feel even the wish to talk. Our day had been one of too delightful a character to often recur, and bright enough to counterbalance weeks of fatigue and inconvenience. As the shades of night closed in upon us, we, by accident, left our track, and, at length, wholly lost our way.

After wandering for some time, we descried a fire on the plain, at a considerable distance, and made towards it. Three shepherds were standing near it, and restraining, with difficulty, two enormous wolf-dogs, whom our approach had alarmed and irritated. The appearance of this group was singularly picturesque, and would have made a fine subject for a painting. The shepherds of these immense plains wear an upper dress of sheepskin, with the woolly side outwards, which covers the breast and back, and protects the thighs. These are made of white or black skin, as it may be; two of the present party had white, the other black; two of them were armed with long Spanish guns, for the protection of their flocks, and the other had the ancient crook. Their dogs were of a dun or mouse-colour, smooth-haired, partaking, in the form of their heads, both of the bull and mastiff, and both taller, and every way larger than any I ever saw in England. We had disturbed the whole party, and their looks of surprise and inquiry, together with the fierce and eager attitude of their dogs, not a little increased the effect. One of them, good-naturedly, came a few hundred yards with us, to set us in the right road; and, finding it late, we spurred quickly home, well pleased with all our adventures, not excepting that, which had arisen from our losing our way, and delayed our return.

The autumnal season, in Estremadura, is proverbially unhealthy, and numbers of the inhabitants die annually of the alarming fever which prevails in the dreaded month of September. The unwholesome vapours, which arise from the beds of the many stagnant pools scattered over the surface of these plains, and always dried up by the summer heats, are said to produce this evil. Be this as it may, towards the end of September, this insidious and resistless enemy found his way into our tranquil quarters, crowded our hospitals with sick, and filled the chapel vaults with victims, over whom we gloomily and sullenly mourned. We would have resigned them in the field of battle, perhaps, with a sigh, yet not without some proud feeling of consolation; but here, to see the cheek blanched, and the arm unnerved by disease, was a constant source of affliction and despondency. There is nothing about which Englishmen are so generally incredulous, or to which they appear so indifferent, as any report touching the danger of a season or a climate, and the approach of sickness; and mortality; for this very reason, when once an alarming disease appears among them, they are overcome with surprise, they lose all elasticity of spirit, hope forsakes them, and they sink unresistingly to the grave. This does not proceed altogether from weakness of character on the bed of sickness, the English soldier thinks more seriously of death, and his accountability hereafter, than perhaps any other, if we except the Protestant soldiers of the north of Germany.

The inhabitants of the south of Europe, and the men who compose the mass of the continental armies, are, for the most part, members of the Roman or Greek church; and, certain it is, that on the bed of death all of these religious persuasions do appear to entertain a confidence of salvation, which, to the sober-minded and humble Protestant, however, innocent and happy a feeling, seems mistaken, if not presumptuous. Strong in youth and health, and of a sanguine disposition, I took my daily exercise, under a burning sun, with very little apprehension. Sometimes, indeed, the passing corpse, and the painful sight of its destruction in the vault, would give a momentary chill to my blood. A very few hours after death, the Spaniards, in that province, are carried to the chapel, cast into the vault, their bodies immediately broken with staves, quick lime thrown upon them, and they are soon utterly consumed; This is well—as it should be, I believe; and, in a hot climate, a most necessary precaution against the danger of infection; but to us, accustomed as we were to a decent interment, and a closed coffin, the practice was, at first, revolting.

On the fourth of October, our division, commanded by General Hill, was reviewed on the plain near Montigo, by Lord Wellington. We had a league to march to the ground, and were kept under arms a considerable time before his Lordship arrived. I was in the highest possible spirits, eager to behold the hero, and as he passed very slowly down the line, observing the men with a keen scrutinizing look, I had the fullest opportunity for indulging my curiosity. I was much struck with his countenance; and, in his quick-glancing eye, prominent nose, and pressed lip, saw, very distinctly marked, the ready presence of mind, and imperturbable decision of character, so essential in a leader, and by which the name of this great commander has been rendered so deservedly illustrious.

I returned home after the review, passed a most cheerful evening, could talk of nothing but war and Wellington—was that night stretched on the bed of sickness, and, in a few days, lay at the very point of death. Youth, an excellent constitution, and high hopeful spirits, enabled me to rally, and in three weeks I was pronounced convalescent. The old woman of my house, who had passed many an hour, during my illness, before the small shrine of the saint that adorned her bed-room, and had put up daily prayers for the health and conversion of the young heretic, was highly delighted, and considered my recovery as a miraculous proof of her saint's power, and a gratifying one of her own worthiness. For myself during the whole time, I had been supported by an internal feeling of the most cheerful confidence; and anticipating both honour as a soldier, and intellectual pleasure as a traveller, in my prospective service, I was unwilling to believe that I could be cut off before I had tasted of the former, or half-satisfied my thirsting curiosity. Neither is the sick-bed of a soldier lonely or deserted. It is true, the anxious care and tender offices of a mother, and the affectionate solicitude of a sister, are wanting. Those comforts, which at home are sure to be provided for the chamber of an invalid, are wanting. Yet, here, some warm-hearted friend will smooth the pillow for your feverish head; will speak to you in the manly yet feeling language of encouragement; will procure, and often prepare for you some delicacy; and, in the dark and silent hour of evening, will sit quietly by your side, consoling you by affectionate pressures of the hand, for pain and suffering, and watching anxiously that nothing may interrupt or scare your needful slumbers.

Yes,—such a picture is not romantic; in civil life, men have homes, parents, wives, children, brothers, sisters; but in the profession of arms they become dependent upon friends. Nowhere is friendship more true, more warm, more exalted, than in the army; absence from the mother-country, privation, peril, the pursuit and attainment of honour, are so many ties which bind soul to soul, in bonds bright and indestructible. Although out of immediate danger and convalescent, it was thought prudent that I should change the air, and I was ordered, by the staff-surgeon, to Elvas. My colonel, who was also a great invalid, and was going to appear before a medical board at Badajos, took me with him. This board, consisting of physicians to the forces, now changed my destination for Lisbon; telling me that Elvas would have proved my grave, and that the staff-surgeon was highly censurable for having so inconsiderately disposed of me. I had journeyed from Torre Major to Badajos on a bullock-car, occasionally relieving myself by mounting a led horse of the colonel's, who rode himself by my side. From Badajos to Elvas we went in a *cabriolet*; and from thence I had suffered so much by the motion, both of the car and carriage, that I made an effort to proceed on horseback. The accommodation which we met with on two, out of the five nights we passed on the road, is worthy of mention.

It was rather advanced in the day when we left Elvas, proposing to sleep at Estremos, a town about six leagues distant From my extreme debility, however, I was unable to ride at such a pace as would have ensured the accomplishment of our journey before nightfall.

At the distance of two leagues from Estremos, the sun set with the most threatening appearances. A sky heavily overcast; a breathless, yet speaking stillness around us; far off, amid the southern hills, a low muttering sound, that faintly reached us; all foretold a violent autumnal storm. Being both invalids, we felt, not a little anxious about shelter, and spurred forward; but strength was denied me, and I fell on the neck of my horse, nearly fainting: the colonel would not leave me, and bidding me recline on my saddle, made his groom lead my animal by the bridle.

Here you may frequently travel from one town to another without passing a village, a country-house, a cottage, or indeed a human being. No clean ale-house as in England; no rustic *auberge*, as in France, invites you to refreshment and repose. If you are benighted, and the weather be fine, you must betake yourself to the first tree: if it be stormy, and you have no baggage or conveniences for encamping, you must wander on. Luckily, however, for us, we espied a light at some distance from the road, and made towards it. It proceeded from a solitary cottage; and a woman, who answered to our knocks, expressed her willingness to receive us. Wretched as was her appearance, I never saw more cordial, more fearless hospitality: she heaped up her little fire, killed, and stewed for us two out of the few chickens she had, spread for us two straw mattresses near the hearth, and regarded us the while with looks of the most benevolent pleasure. Seated on a rude bench of cork, near this cottage fire, I thankfully partook of the repast she prepared; and while the thunder burst in peals the most loud and awful over our heads, and the pouring rain beat rudely on her humble dwelling, with a heartfelt sensation of gratitude I composed myself to rest.

Comfort is ever comparative; and, after all, if his wishes be moderate, how little does man require! Sick, hungry, and exhausted, I wanted shelter, food, and repose: I enjoyed all these blessings; the storm raged without, but not a raindrop fell on me. I never ate with a keener relish, I never passed a night in more sweet or refreshing slumbers. Yet where, let me ask, was the hotel in England which, in the caprice of sickness, would have satisfied all my wants and wishes? When we rose with the morning to depart, our good hostess was resolute in refusing any remuneration, though the wretched appearance of her hovel, and the rags on her children, bespoke the extreme of poverty.

"No," said she; "the saints guided you to my threshold, and I thank them. My husband, too, was journeying yesterday, perhaps last night, amid that thunder-storm; he also knocked at some Christian's door, and found shelter."

We caught one of the children outside, and forcing some dollars into its little hands, mounted, and rode off. I shall never forget that night, or that speech; and no sermon on the charities of life could be more instructive.

At Estremos I was obliged to give up all idea of riding farther, and was borne the rest of my journey on a creaking bullock-car. We stopped for one night at a common *posada*, about five leagues from Aldea Gallega, the town where, in travelling down by this route, you generally embark on the Tagus, and cross to Lisbon. This *posada* is a building, in size and appearance not much unlike an English barn. It is very simply divided. Below is stabling for fifty or sixty mules or more; and at the farthest extremity, without any partition between it and the space allotted to the animals, is the kitchen. Above is a large loft, with one or two corners boarded off, dignified with the name of chambers, and furnished with dirty mattresses and iron lamps. The stable was filled with mules, the kitchen with muleteers, and the loft with vermin; yet here, for want of better accommodation, were we compelled to pass the night; I need hardly add, it was a sleepless one. People of any rank or condition in life, both in Spain and Portugal, when necessitated to make journeys, always lodge in private houses, to which they gain admittance, either by regular billets, recommendations, or by hiring chambers for the night. These *posadas*, of which I speak, are seldom resorted to by any but muleteers; for whose accommodation, and to more equally divide the journeys of their trains, we often find them built in spots two or three leagues from any town or village.

The life of the muleteer is very hardy, and pretty much the same in all parts of the Peninsula. He is exposed to all weathers, for he is ever on the road. Each individual has the charge of three or four mules; and the labour of loading and unloading them daily, and foraging for them, is not trifling. The food of the muleteer is coarse; a large dish of chick-pease, boiled with a morsel of pork; a sausage, or some dry salt fish, fried in strong oil, are his most common and favourite dishes. He drinks more than the Spanish peasant, and generally carries a large leathern bottle or bag, filled with wine. He never undresses at night, but sleeps either in the stable with his mules, or on the floor of the kitchen; indeed, in the summer, more generally in the open air, for he often bivouacs. In all places, a pack-saddle is his pillow, and a mule-cloth his coverlet He is an honest, good-tempered, cheerful creature, and you almost always hear him singing on the road. A train of mules is seldom less than fifty; but it is not uncommon to meet two or three trains, or more, travelling the same road, and laden with the same merchandise. Each train has its captain or leader, who is invariably a trust-worthy man of the best character.

CHAPTER 6

We Meet the Spanish Army

Two days after my arrival in Lisbon, I suffered a severe relapse, and was for six weeks confined to my bed, during one of which my life was altogether despaired of. To nature, and a most careful attendant, I was indebted for that favourable change, which medicine had in vain laboured to produce. This attendant, a valuable private servant of my colonel's, was placed over me by him, with orders never to leave me till I died or recovered: though himself a delicate invalid, he had resigned what he most wanted to my service. Such kindness I can never forget; and life, preserved to me by such generous friendship, became an increased blessing.

To feel yourself daily regaining health and strength is, under all circumstances, delightful. At Lisbon, the period of my convalescence glided away with the most pleasing rapidity. I dined daily in a most agreeable society; I passed my mornings in studying the Portuguese and Spanish languages; and oftentimes, of an evening, muffled up as an invalid, I stole, in a *cabriolet*, to the theatre of San Carlos, or to the Opera Buffa, and enjoyed the sweet music of Portugallo, and the pleasing voices and admirable acting of Vaccani and Scarameli.

Lisbon too, at the beginning of the year 1810, independent of its usual gaiety as a metropolis and a large commercial city, presented a novel and interesting spectacle. The note of preparation had already sounded, and it was well known that the invasion of Portugal, a measure long and avowedly contemplated by

France, could not be far distant. The French armies, victorious in the field of Ocaña, had burst through the vaunted defiles of the Sierra Morena, entered Seville, Cordova, Jaen, and Grenada, without resistance, and two corps were actually blockading Cadiz, the last and only refuge of the patriot government. The most active operations were carrying on in Catalonia by Suchet; and troops from the corps of Ney, then stationed between the Tormes and the Douro, were marched against Leon and Asturias, with a view to the complete and secure reduction of those important provinces. It was plain, however, that though the armies of France, aided by skill, courage, and discipline, could march triumphantly from the Pyrenees to the Pillars of Hercules; and though they held the capital for the Usurper, and overawed both the Castiles; still it was plain, that. they could never hope effectually to subdue Spain, or even to retain possession of it, until they had subjugated Portugal, and driven out British soldiers from her camps, and British influence from her cabinet.

The clouds were already gathering, and the storm was distinctly foretold; submitting themselves to the able guidance, and prudent counsels of their faithful, and more experienced allies, the Portuguese manfully girded their loins for the contest, and resolved bravely to abide the issue of a struggle. The discipline of their army was daily improving. The uncommon exertions of Marshal Beresford, and the British officers under him, were rewarded by the praises of all who witnessed the miraculous change in the appearance, movement, and general conduct of the soldiers committed to their charge. The old, incorrigibly indolent, and useless Portuguese officers were placed on the retired list, and their commissions were given to young men, full of zeal, willing to learn, and able to discharge the active duties required of them. The streets of Lisbon glittered with uniforms; the shop-windows of all the embroiderers furnished a grand display of military ornaments. The magazines of the gun-smiths and the sword-cutlers were constantly filled with customers: even the peaceful merchants formed themselves into corps, and volunteered to perform the duties of the garrison. These corps, both horse and foot, were most handsomely clothed and appointed; their cavalry wore hussar jackets of brown, covered with gold lace, and were, generally speaking, well mounted. The commercial regiment of infantry furnished a grand guard, daily, near the exchange. I often attended the parading and mounting of their duties, all which was conducted in the most orderly and soldier-like manner. Their band was excellent; it was composed entirely of professed musicians, and they were all masters of the instruments on which they performed. I have had the good fortune to hear many very fine bands; never any, however, superior to this.

There were, as may be supposed, in the ranks of these commercial corps, many awkward and uncouth figures; but any disposition to smile at them was immediately repressed by the reflection that they might, perhaps, in the hour of approaching peril, be called upon to prove the sincerity of their patriotism, and the nature of their respect for those sacred obligations, which a voluntary drawing of the sword had imposed on them.

About the close of the month of March, being perfectly restored to health, I rejoined my regiment. The corps of General Hill, to which it was attached, lay at this time distributed in cantonments in the province of Alemtejo. The general's head-quarters were established at Portalegre, in which city two brigades and a half of the second division of infantry were quartered: My regiment lay detached in Alegrete, a small town, most romantically situated, in a wild and picturesque country, about three leagues from Portalegre, in the direction of Albuquerque. My journey to the army had quite the character of an excursion for pleasure. We had a small agreeable party, all convalescents from sickness; and having benefited a little by experience, we carried with us many little comforts and conveniences we had the last year neglected or despised.

We proceeded up the Tagus by water to Abrantes, sleeping every night in some town or village on the banks of the river; and, from Abrantes, we, in four days, reached our destination. The soft season of the year, the mild balmy air, the rich verdure, and the various fruit-trees, clothed in their beauteous blossoms, all contributed to beguile any sense of fatigue; and I seemed, on the day of my arrival, to have made no exertion since I left Lisbon; Alas! when I came again to stand on the parade, for how many a face did my eye inquire in vain:—in the space of four short months, my regiment had buried nearly three hundred men, all in the prime of life, and vigour of their manhood. They had all fallen victims to the sickly season, in Spanish Estremadura. The officers of the army had not suffered in proportion to the men, as they were enabled to live more generously; for, at that time, wine and spirits were never issued regularly to the soldiers; and the wine, which was occasionally procured for them, was very indifferent. There was, moreover, a very great scarcity of bark in the regimental hospitals, and numbers perished for the want of it. Some powerful reason of a political or military nature, doubtless, caused Lord Wellington to occupy and maintain a position, which proved so cruelly fatal to the health and efficiency of his small army.

April, May, and June we remained stationary: once, indeed, we broke up, and bivouacked for a couple of nights about two leagues in advance, in consequence of some slight demonstration made by a moveable column belonging to the *corps d'armée* of Regnier, then commanding in Spanish Estremadura, but, the enemy retiring, we returned to our tranquil quarters. There is not a rock, a mountain, a stream, an orange garden, a chapel, a shrine, or a cross near Alegrete, but I know and recollect, and can recall them all. At this very moment that I am writing, at the distance of nearly seven years, I can summon before me the fort, the church, the square, the old priest, the peasants, their wives, their,children. We had become quite domesticated among them; they liked our men, and they were both kind and respectful to the officers. Fond of passing my mornings alone, each day I took my solitary ride or ramble; a practice I think delightful; and which, I find, makes me doubly enjoy society and conversation in the evening.

How strongly does the mind attach itself to any spot, where it has daily resorted to give fancy the rein, and suffered her to range undisturbed through the paths of her own fair creation.

The trees and shrubs are as tender-hearted friends, who have become acquainted with your weakness, but care not to expose it. In one of my walks here, after wandering along the rude and pathless banks of a clear mountain stream, which now leaped, now run, now rippled, now smoothly flowed along its ever-varying bed, I arrived at a small romantic chapel, such a one as you often find in the Peninsula, a league or more from any human habitation. In the shade, near the door, I observed a small basket, apparently filled only with the most beautiful flowers; I approached to take one;—when stooping, I beheld a lovely infant about a year old; it was dressed prettily and tastefully; though pale, I thought it slept, for its paleness did not appear as of death; it was, however, cold and lifeless, yet it had nothing of the corpse, nothing of the grave about it. I kissed its delicate fair face, and thought, not without a sigh, on its parents. A voice startled me, and turning, I beheld a decent-looking peasant woman, with an old man, and two or three children from ten to fifteen years of age—"Are you the mother of this babe?" said I.

"Yes, *Señor.*"

"I pity you from my heart"—

"How so, *Señor?* To have borne and buried a Christian, without sin, I look on as a blessing, and I praise the Holy Virgin that she has vouchsafed to take him to herself."—

I gazed earnestly at the woman. Was this insensibility? or was it enthusiastic reverence for, and pious resignation to, the will of God? — I decided for the latter; for I saw her bend over her child with an expression of countenance rapturously affectionate. I knelt down, once more, to read its innocent features.—Yes, there was the charm: remorse, fear, and doubt, could not be traced there. All was innocence, and purity, and truth.—"Your child," said I, "my good woman, is perhaps ere now, a cherubim in heaven."

"*Señor*, you cannot be a heretic?"

"No, I am a Christian of another sect."

"Ah, you must be a Christian; I thought so, but the priests said you English were all heretics."

So much for priests and peasants. The breach between the Roman Catholic and the Protestant church has certainly been rendered unnaturally, if not impassably wide, by the stubborn pride and designing policy of a crafty and intolerant priesthood. Though I am here speaking of the Roman Catholic clergy, I cannot but feel that the violence of the early Reformers, who, in detestation of the Romish Church, abrogated many things, defiled, perhaps, by abuse, but decent in themselves, and allowed in the primitive church, very greatly assisted to produce this evil. Do we not, I would ask, in essentials think alike? and is not the grand and blessed scheme of man's redemption, through the mediation of Christ, the first article of belief, and the resting-place of faith with us both? I certainly, in the course of my residence in Spain, had occasion often to reflect that my countrymen were too apt to confound the errors and abuses of the church government among the Roman Catholics, with the belief and practices of their religion.

But to return to my recollections.—In one of my rides, about two leagues from the cantonment, as I was stopping to water my mule in a mill-stream, I heard on the opposite bank the sound of voices, loud and cheerful as in song, and, at intervals, a note of the guitar. Riding forward through the trees, I soon came upon an open green, where I found about a hundred villagers, assembled near a small chapel to celebrate the festival of San Domingo. The mass was over, and they were all seated on the ground, refreshing themselves with cakes and wine. They were in their holiday dresses, and those dresses were for the most part exceedingly picturesque. At my first appearance there was a dead silence; they looked as if they dreaded some news which might break up their happy meeting; or, at all events, as if they knew me for an Englishman, and disliked my intrusion; but when I dismounted, and throwing myself on the ground among them, asked to be allowed to share their mirth and happiness, no words can describe their delighted cordiality. I had so accustomed myself to converse with the peasantry, that we soon became familiar, and I passed with them six very pleasant hours. After their light repast, the best of which was spread before me and a Capuchin friar, they rose to dance; and though there was nothing graceful in their style of moving, still the total novelty of the picture, the dresses, the singing, the guitars, the cork-trees, and the chapel, produced a very pleasing effect; and could the curtain of Drury Lane rise and discover such a scene and such a group, the applause would know no bounds.

Amid this festive party there was one very pretty girl, with fair blue eyes and a blooming complexion, beauties very uncommon in Portugal, and these the conscious damsel had artfully contrived to set off, by a black hat, lined with pink silk, and a pretty well-fancied dress. Her mother, who seemed very proud of her, asked me, if she would really be considered a pretty, girl among Englishwomen? and on my assuring her, that I had never yet seen the spot where she would not be considered very handsome, the old woman turning quickly, said, "Ah, *Señor*, where shall I conceal her from shame and insult, when the French come again to ravage our country?"

"Let us hope" said I, "that God may enable us to defend your country."

She made no reply, but shook her head mournfully: I repressed a sigh, and immediately turned the conversation; for why should idle anticipation of tomorrow's misery be suffered to cloud the innocent gaiety of today? They broke up at sunset, and all returned peaceably to their homes, without noise, quarrelling, or intoxication. I am free to confess, that I very much admire the manners and customs of these happy peasants, nor have I ever subscribed to that prejudiced opinion, which affects to condemn or despise them as senseless and frivolous.

On the 30th of June, our regiment was called in from its advanced station, and joined its brigade in the town of Portalegre, and our appearances justified the belief, that the campaign was about to open. We remained for twelve days here; I was very fortunate in my billet. My host, a mild, well informed, venerable old canon, gave me most excellent apartments, and a free access to a little cabinet, in which he had a pretty selection of

French authors, and some very handsome editions of the classics. The windows of my chamber commanded a most enchanting prospect, and I had no want or wish unsatisfied, if I except the natural anxiety I always felt to take the field, and gain the proud experience of a soldier.

At this time the corps of Junot and Ney, under the orders of Massena, occupied positions on or near the Agueda; the troops of Ney, indeed, were carrying on the siege of Ciudad Rodrigo. Regnier, with the second corps of the French army, lay cantoned in Spanish Estremadura, in a state of the most active preparation, appearing to menace and watch us in Alemtejo.

On the 13th of July, we marched to a camp near Alpalhâo, where we halted five days, waiting until Regnier, who was then drawing near the Tagus, should cross that river, in order that we might make an immediate and corresponding movement. We were here all reviewed, and I had the satisfaction of seeing, for the first time, a large division of Portuguese under arms. The men were remarkably fine, and, considering the short time that had elapsed since their organization, in very high order. Twenty-four regiments of the line, six of light infantry, ten of cavalry, together with a due proportion of excellent artillery, then composed the native army of Portugal: their effective strength might be about thirty-five thousand; of this number, however, many regiments were not yet in a sufficient state of forwardness to take the field, and remained therefore in garrisons. The total force of British and Portuguese in the field, including Hill's corps, could not have exceeded fifty-eight thousand; of these twenty-five thousand were Portuguese. About eight thousand British, and six thousand Portuguese, composed the command of General Hill. All the other divisions of the army were under the immediate orders of Lord Wellington, and lay most ably distributed, opposite the main French force commanded by Massena.

My object, however, is not to give a professional sketch of the campaigns, but to present to the reader as faithfully as I can the varieties and pleasures of a life on active service, as they deeply impressed me, though more perhaps as a traveller, and a man of feeling, than as a scientific soldier. Not that I was indifferent to the interest which every intelligent mind must take in extensive military operations, and in seeing war carried on on a grand scale, throughout a series of brilliant campaigns; but although I was provided with good maps, although eager in my inquiries, intimate with some clever and communicative staff officers, and, from a long habit of military reading, often just, or rather fortunate in my conclusions, still I felt and feel, that, after all, the best information of a regimental officer of humble rank must be very imperfect.

It is a great misfortune for the British army which served in the Peninsula, and for the Duke of Wellington himself, that no man, possessed of the necessary information, and the ability to work upon his materials, has been found to give a correct and valuable history of their campaigns. It is quite idle to send the official documents and papers required for such a work to the most able writer, and acknowledged historian of the day. Such a man, however great his talents, however nervous and rich his language, is, and must be, ill-qualified to write a military work, if he be a civilian, unacquainted with armies, and has never served; he may indeed succeed in painting the noble struggles of a patriotic population, he may describe in a glowing strain of manly eloquence such a defence as that of Saragossa, or the courageous exploits of Mountain-Guerillas; but he can never impart to an account of the operations of regular, armies, that charm and interest it is certainly capable of receiving; he will find writing on the subject at all, a laborious and painful task, and will, after all, perhaps, produce a book, the dry perusal of which disappoints himself, and satisfies no one.—No.—A man must, like a Xenophon, or a Polybius, march with an army before he ventures to become the historian of its exploits. Would that some division general with the pen of a Burgoyne, or a Hutchinson, had marched and fought with the British troops in the Peninsula!

But to return to our camp. On July 18th, we again broke up, and marching by Niza, towards the Tagus, crossed that river at Villa Velha, and pursued our route through Sarnadas, and Castello Branco, to Atalaya, a considerable village situated at the very foot of that magnificent range of mountains called the Sierra de Estrella, to the north of which lay our main force under the orders of Wellington. Instructed by our last year's wants, our officers now took the field very comfortably provided; many of us were mounted, most of us carried tents, and experience having shewn us what would be really useful, we had, at our leisure, procured and planned many little camp conveniences. Myself and my companion had our tent, camp-table, and stools, *paillasses*, canteen, &c., and, after our servants got accustomed to the life, provided the weather was fair, and no especial order of march, or readiness, interfered, our meals were prepared and served in bivouacs, the most rude and unfrequented, altogether remote from towns or cities, with the greatest regularity, cleanliness, and comfort. A quarter of an hour after the halt of the column, our tent was pitched, kettle boiled, breakfast-cloth spread, and tea-things laid out under some shady tree, the goats milked, and we were seated in comfort at our cheerful meal. The dinner, too, no great variety in the cookery to be sure, for there are but two dukes seen in a camp, namely, soup and *bouillé*, or an Irish stew, but these with rice, pumpkin, tomatoes, and a bottle of good country wine, left a moderate man little to wish for, and nothing to grumble at.

At the bivouack, near Villa Velha, we took up our ground within a mile of a Spanish division under the orders of General Carrera, which was, marching to Badajos. This was a remarkably fine body of men, though completely disorganized by defeat, and almost disheartened by the absence of that hope and encouragement which success can, alone, effectually inspire. They had been present at the fatal affair of Alba de Tormes, and had now just witnessed the fall of Ciudad Rodrigo. Upon us they appeared to look with a contempt, which their ignorance as soldiers, and their zeal as Spaniards, made in some measure, excusable. They knew little, if any thing, about the regular practice of war; they only knew that we had not fired a shot by their side, since the battle of Talavera; that our companions in arms under

Sir John Moore had fled through the strong country of Gallicia, without fighting, two years before, and their angry and contemptuous looks told us plainly, that they expected we should retire through Portugal on the advance of Massena, with similar precipitation. I was vexed to observe all this, but made great allowances for the natural irritation of their feelings, under so much national distress and danger, and found it in my heart to forgive them. Carrera, the general who commanded them, sat under some trees with a party of their superior officers, smoking a cigar: his head was uncovered, and he had on a light undress waistcoat: he was a strikingly handsome man; as our well-appointed troops filed past this spot towards their ground, he regarded them with the most silent and provoking haughtiness. He was not a man of any talent, but he was a young, ardent, intrepid soldier, and a true friend to his country. In the year 1811 or 1812, he fell in the streets of Murcia, covered with sabre wounds, having maintained for a short time a most unequal struggle with five French dragoons. I mention the meeting with this Spanish division with a view to show how they were often led, and how little system and method there was in the march,, and movements of men, who, I should have said, were scattered through their bivouack, without any regularity of formation, or any appearance of discipline and control, and subjected to the orders of generals, perhaps impelled in most cases by patriotism, but seldom governed, or even enlightened, by judgement

In the town of Castello Branco there is little remarkable. Its citadel and walls are in a state of ruin and decay. Although not fortified, it is still very important, as a military station, for the country round it, especially on the grand road which passes by Sobreira Formosa towards the Zezere, and abounds in strong and defensible positions: it has been also formerly a Roman station; and wherever we can trace the awful vestiges of those all-conquering soldiers, the Roman legions, we feel, I think, a very exalted and indefinable satisfaction. From our camp near Atalaya, the eye ranged over the southern face of the proud Sierra d'Estrella, rising many thousand feet above the level of the sea, traversed by good roads, formed with infinite labour over clefts of rocks, and gemmed with several white towns and villages, which lie nestling and sparkling on its ample bosom. We remained here eight days, three of which it rained incessantly, and with great violence. A bivouack in heavy weather does not, I allow, present a very comfortable appearance. The officers sit shivering in their wet tents, idle, and angry till dinner time, after which they generally contrive to kill the evening with mulled wine, round a camp-kettle lid filled with hot wood-ashes, by way of a fire. The men with their forage caps drawn over their ears, huddle together under banks or walls, or crowd round cheerless, smoky fires, cursing their commissaries, the rain, and the French. When, however, the clouds rolled away, and the sun shone forth again in all its splendour, again was spread before us the grand prospect of the Estrella, ever the same, yet ever varying; for who shall paint the bright and changing hues, which, at the rise and set of sun, visit scenes like these?

CHAPTER 7

Action at Buzaco

On the thirtieth we marched from Atalaya, carrying with us, I remember, a good supply of the delicious wine of Alpedrinha, a mountain village about a league from our camp. We halted for the night at Tenelhas, and the following day marched for Sazedas, a small town, with a fine position near it for a camp. As we did not get our orders to march from the bivouack at Tenelhas until late in the afternoon, we did not expect to reach our ground before night-fall; for large bodies of troops, encumbered with artillery and baggage, of necessity, move slow, but, as not unfrequently happened, the troops were halted for the night, right and left of the road, in the formation of march: no baggage, no cloaks, no supper; but an uncomfortable, fitful, broken dog-sleep, in a heavy dew. I give both sides of the picture; because the pleasures and joys of any life, as they exist only by comparison, so they can arise only out of its varieties. We halted until the seventeenth of August at Sazedas, where the division was regularly and comfortably hutted.

Whenever we remained a week or a fortnight stationary, the sutlers who followed the army overtook and opened their temporary shops in the towns near us, or in our very camps; and thus we were often well, though dearly, supplied with many comforts, such as tea, sugar, brandies, wines, *segars*, &c. In these sort of camps, we felt two serious wants, I allow; books, and the society of women. It is true that in the Peninsula we never enjoyed either the one or the other in perfection; yet in quarters we could often procure a few odd volumes of Latin or French, which served to beguile, and often usefully to occupy our time; and for female society you frequently met with agreeable and interesting girls in your billet. Indeed I remember at Portalegre we used to frequent the grates of two nunneries, and all the sisters seemed flattered by our attentions. A military band was often brought down to the outer court of their sacred prisons, for their amusement, and some of the officers would sit for hours in the convent parlours, talking with the nuns, whom a double row of thick gratings, so contrived that you could only shake hands in the space between the two rows, separated from their, gay *inamoratas*. Some of these unfortunates were young and engaging: one, a very pretty interesting girl, in the convent of Santa Clara, died before we left the city. She was passionately in love with a British officer, who was himself at the time much affected by her loss. I considered her death a mercy; for she must have either lived a life of hopeless misery, or dared to rend asunder the sacred tie which bound her to her country, her family, and her convent, and have survived, perhaps, after all, the very flame to which she had so innocently given birth.

In another convent in that city, I remember a sister, neither young nor beautiful, but so interesting as to rivet attention and to awaken all one's sympathy. She was not always herself; and when in the fit of her strange melancholy, she would come to the grate and sing; sweetly indeed, but with a wildness, that filled the eyes of those who heard her with tears. She never wept herself; but smiled often, and most mournfully. She had been disappointed in love early in life, and sent into the convent; at least we heard so. I should like to have known her history; but on this she never spoke, and I respected her sorrow too much to pain her by an unguarded question. She was very fond of the English officers: in whose countenances, at least in many, she might have observed an expression of manly pity, which soothed perhaps her wounded heart.

But, if such opportunities of occupying the mind and indulging the feelings were not to be met with in a camp, still it had its peculiar pleasures. You rose with the sun daily, and you had a fine martial scene constantly before your eyes; you walked and rode through a beautiful country, planning schemes of future happiness, or cherishing natural (it matters not how vain) hopes of future distinction: nor is the precious *"Far niente"* to be forgotten; for it is not necessary to have the genius, or the passion of Rousseau, to appreciate this enjoyment. All persons who have feeling and fancy, know how delightful are the unconnected and confused reveries of solitude, and the idle exercise of thought The romantic scenery of the Peninsula assists and promotes such feelings. Often too, in our camps, we received papers and letters from dear old England, and our eager politicians assembled round the appointed tent or tree, allotted as our news-room. Often would we dine together, in small convivial parties, to talk over past scenes, and future prospects. At times, as the sun set, and the shades of evening fell around us, walking on some upland near the camp, you might catch the mellowed and softened tones of a distant band, breathing forth some sweet and touching air, with which you had been from boyhood acquainted.

Oh, memory! how pure, how exquisite, are thy pleasures!: To thee, and to thy sister Hope, the bright handmaids who support us through the rude path of existence, how deeply are all men indebted!

On the seventeenth of August, our battalion and another were moved to a camp at San Domingo, about five miles in advance of Sazedas, as a support to some light infantry and cavalry, which lay detached in front of us again, occupying Castello Branco and the adjacent villages. Our bivouack here was a very delightful one: the trees were large and beautiful; a most transparent brook of sweet water ran past our lines; and the men were hutted with great comfort, neatness, and regularity. Our general occupied a small chapel by the road side, the only building near us; and peasants from the distance of two or three leagues, hearing that our discipline was strict, and that we paid liberally for every thing, soon established a market in our camp, and brought us constant supplies of bread, milk, eggs, poultry, honey, and excellent country wine. He who has fed on coarse ration beef and hard biscuit, and that for two or three weeks at a time, will express no surprise at my noticing these trifles; and he who has never served, may smile at the mention of them, provided he does so with good humour, and ends by excusing me.

While we remained here an affair of cavalry took place in front of us, in which some of our 13th Light Dragoons captured a foraging party of the enemy. The prisoners were marched past our ground to headquarters. I had never as yet, though upwards of a year in the country, seen a French soldier; and I walked out alone to meet the escort I know not how it was, but I had certainly connected very strange ideas with the appearance of the French soldiery. What I expected to see I cannot at all define; not, certainly, men of fair, fresh complexions, tall, well made, and handsome. Such, however, were the prisoners: they were *chasseurs*, about sixty in number, clothed in neat green uniforms, with very becoming forage-caps. Some of them seemed cast down and depressed, a few irritated and indignant; but the greater part gazed around them with fearless and careless curiosity, while their laughing blue eyes certainly indicated any thing rather than cruelty. It is true these men were very few of them natives of France; but although Germans, they were soldiers of the French army marched with it, fought with it, and were enemies whom we often encountered. Much of Napoleon's cavalry was composed of Germans; and the very numbered regiments of France, of all arms, contained Italians, Belgians, Dutch, and other foreigners.[9] They were, therefore, samples of the foe with whom we were to contend.

Among them, indeed, was one man, whose horrible and ferocious countenance I shall never forget. He was of the mid-

---

9. Though the detachment here named was composed of Germans, I must say from subsequent experience that I have never seen finer men than among the native troops of France. We certainly have, in England, strange prejudices even about the personal appearance of Frenchmen; nor are they at all confined to the lowest classes; few Englishmen of education are at all prepared, when they first cross the channel, for the sight of such fine, athletic, well-formed men, as are often to be met with in France.

dle size, stout, and muscular; the hair of his head and his immense *moustachios* were perfectly white, his face pale, his eyes small and somewhat red, and the expression of his look was at once unnatural and pitiless. His fellow-soldiers seemed to shun him; and on my questioning them, I found that he was a native of some province dependant upon Austria. His language, they said, was hardly intelligible to them: he was quite a savage, they added; but a brave one, and good food for powder. I shuddered at the very thought that such a man should be a soldier. To such a wretch, thought I, the weeping female would kneel in vain: the smile of the helpless babe, the groan of the wounded warrior, would never stay that uplifted arm. He was the only individual of the party wounded, for there had been little, if any resistance; but such a man was to be disabled, before he could be disarmed.

On the second of September, our battalion returned to Sazedas; on the twelfth we broke up, and marched upon Sobreira Formosa, where we halted for five days. Though the face of the country was mountainous, the weather was oppressively hot: we were, however, protected by spreading horse-chestnuts, the finest, I think, I ever saw.

A Portuguese division was encamped here, very near us: at their evening parade, I walked down their line. The time seemed fast approaching, when we might probably fight side by side; and, on their efficiency, the possibility of prolonging the glorious struggle in the Peninsula, would very greatly depend. The grenadiers of the brigade of Algarve particularly attracted my notice: they were all fine-sized, soldier-like men; and their brown complexions, black *moustachios*, and large dark eyes, gave them a truly martial appearance. I here, for the first time, heard them sing their evening hymn: the companies were formed in circles round their officers at sunset, and chaunted forth this their evening service in a strain which was, to me, alike novel, solemn, and pleasing.

On the morning of the seventeenth, we were again put in motion, and marched rapidly to the Mondego, on the southern bank of which, somewhere near the Ponte de Murcella, we halted. In our route we crossed the Zezere, near Villa del Rey; our bivouack near which town was wretched in the extreme. It rained in torrents, and the tent was hardly any protection: thunder too, and lightning, which frightened our cattle, and a high wind beating against our canvass, completed our misery. And yet with a mind amused and spirits elated we suffer little, and these discomforts are felt as nothing. I well recollect my companion mulled some wine for me, and I afterwards crept under my blankets, and throwing an oil-cloth over me, contrived to forget the tempest and its miseries, in a very sound and uninterrupted sleep. With the sun I rose; and what a change to reward us! The morning was heavenly, the weather mild, the trees and fields all glittering with rain-drops, and the face of nature looked gay and refreshed. Our march for the first two leagues, after fording the Zezere, lay through a very pretty country, well cultivated, with many neat-looking cottages and vineyards, all blushing with fruit. As we passed along, the peasants brought out wine and peaches, plums and grapes, selling cheaply to the officers, and giving fruit generously to many of the men for nothing. We encamped near some fine plantations of fir on that night, and made large and most brilliant fires: the next evening, just as we had halted and began cooking, we received orders to march forward again in an hour, and continued in motion the whole night, over very bad roads, which greatly delayed the guns, and rendered our march a slow and fatiguing one.

Our men had received lately rather a short allowance of bread; and although they were all gaiety and good humour, this. forced march a little tired them. I shall never forget the speech of one of our men to his comrade, as they toiled on stumbling in the dark just before me, and it certainly does describe a soldier's share of campaigning very wittily:

"Bill," said he, "the parliament and the great men at home, they do know all about the movements of the army and the *grandè* lord, but they don't know any thing about *indivijals* (individuals); for instance, now, they don't know that you are damned tired, and that I hae got no *pong*"[10] (*paõ*). There is more in such a speech than at first strikes upon the ear, and the man of reflection might philosophise on it with advantage.

We took up our ground near a small village behind the Sierra de Murcella, on the twenty-third, and remained three days stationary; our picquets occupying posts on the very crests of those stupendous mountains, and overlooking an immense and beautiful tract of country to the north-east. I was twenty-four hours at one of these posts. Unless the elevation of a mountain is so considerable, as to enable you to look down upon the country below you, as upon a map drawn by nature, I confess I am no great admirer of what are termed open and extensive prospects: the eye is strained and fatigued, and the fancy never much delighted. But here, to look down upon the winding course of the calm and tranquil Mondego, and to watch the romantic Alva hurrying gladly along to pour its tributary waters into her peaceful bosom, was a scene beautiful, as rare. Could a day pass heavily where the eye might rest on such a landscape? impossible!—Nor is a night on outline picquet without its charms: when all around, or near you is hushed and silent; when no sound meets the ear, but the soft foot-fall of your watchful sentries,—the mind, rejoicing in its freedom, and undiverted by any outward objects, looks in upon itself with grateful rapture. All is still, yet you seem to listen to many a well-known voice; all is dark, yet the features of the absent, whom you love, beam brightly upon you, and happy and distant scenes rise busily before you, and gild these lonely hours with pleasures the most enviable, and the most refined.

On the twenty-sixth we again moved, and fording the Mondego, climbed the lofty Sierra de Buzaco; and found ourselves on the right of Wellington's army, and in order of battle. Our position extended nearly eight miles along this mountainous and rocky ridge, and the ground on which we formed inclin-

10. "*Paõ*,"—in Portuguese, "bread." The English. soldiers vulgarly pronounced it "pong."

ing with a slope to our own rear, most admirably concealed both the disposition and the numbers of our force. My regiment had no sooner piled arms, than I walked to the verge of the mountain on which we lay, in the hope that I might discover something of the enemy. Little, however, was I prepared for the magnificent scene which burst on my astonished sight Far as the eye could stretch, the glittering of steel, and clouds of dust raised by cavalry and artillery, proclaimed the march of a countless army; while, immediately below me, at the feet of those precipitous heights on which I stood, their picquets were already posted; thousands of them were already halted in their bivouacs, and column too after column, arriving in quick succession, reposed upon the ground allotted to them, and swelled the black and enormous masses.

The numbers of the enemy were, at the lowest calculation, seventy-five thousand, and this host formed in three distinct and heavy columns; while to the rear of their left, at a more considerable distance, you might see a large encampment of their cavalry, and the whole country behind them seemed covered with their train, their ambulance, and their commissariat. This, then, was a French army: here lay, before me, the men who had once, for nearly two years, kept the whole coast of England in alarm; who had conquered Italy, overrun Austria, shouted victory on the plains of Austerlitz, and humbled, in one day, the power, the pride, and the martial renown of Prussia, on the field of Jena. Tomorrow, methought, I may, for the first time, hear the din of battle, behold the work of slaughter, share the honours of a hard-fought field, or be numbered with the slain. I returned slowly to the line; and, after an evening passed in very interesting and animated conversation, though we had neither baggage nor fires, we lay down, rolled in our cloaks, and with the stony surface of the mountain for our bed, and the sky for our canopy, slept or thought away the night.

Two hours before break of day, the line was under arms; but the two hours glided by rapidly and silently. At last, just as the day dawned, a few distant shots were heard on our left, and were soon followed by the discharge of cannon and the quick, heavy, and continued roll of musketry. We received orders to move, and support the troops attacked: the whole of Hill's, corps, amounting to fourteen thousand men, was thrown into open column, and moved to its left in: steady double quick, and in the highest order.

When within about a furlong of one of the points of attack, from which the enemy was just then driven by the Seventy-Fourth regiment, I cast my eye back to see if I could discover the rear of our divisions: eleven thousand men were following; all in sight, all in open column, all rapidly advancing in double quick time. No one, but a soldier, can picture to himself such a sight; and it is, even for him, a rare and a grand one. It certainly must have had a very strong effect on such of the enemy as, from the summit of the ridge, which they had most intrepidly ascended, beheld it, and who, ignorant of Hill's presence, thought they had been attacking the extreme of the British right. We were halted exactly in rear of that spot, from which the Seventy-Fourth regiment, having just repulsed a 'column, was retiring in line, with the most beautiful regularity, its colours all torn with shot. Here a few shells flew harmlessly over our line, but we had not the honour of being engaged. The first wounded man I ever beheld in the field was carried past me, at this moment; he was a fine young Englishman, in the Portuguese service, and lay helplessly, in a blanket, with both his legs shattered by cannon-shot. He looked pale, and big drops of perspiration stood on his manly; forehead; but he spoke not—his agony appeared unutterable. I secretly wished him death; a mercy, I believe, that was not very long withheld.

About this time, Lord Wellington, with a numerous staff, galloped up, and delivered his orders to General Hill, immediately in front of our corps; I therefore distinctly overheard him. "If they attempt this point again, Hill, you will give them a volley, and charge bayonets; but don't let your people follow them too far down the hill."

I was particularly struck with the style of this order, so decided, so manly, and breathing no doubt as to the repulse of any attack; it confirmed confidence. Lord Wellington's simplicity of manner in the delivery of orders, and in command, is quite that of an able man. He has nothing of the truncheon about him; nothing full-mouthed, important, or fussy; his orders, on the field, are all short, quick, clear, and to the purpose. The French, however, never moved us throughout the day; their two desperate assaults had been successfully repelled, and their loss, as compared to ours, exceedingly severe. From the ridge, in front of our present ground, we could see them far better than the evening before; arms, appointments, uniforms, were all distinguishable. They occupied themselves in removing their wounded from the foot of our position; but as none of their troops broke up, it was generally concluded that they would renew their attacks on the morrow, In the course of the day, our men. went down to a small brook, which flowed between the opposing armies, for water; and French and English soldiers might be seen drinking out of the same narrow stream, and even leaning over to shake hands with each other. One private of my own regiment, actually exchanged forage-caps with a soldier of the enemy, as a token of regard and goodwill. Such courtesies, if they do not disguise, at least soften the horrid features of war; and it is thus we learn to reconcile our minds to scenes of blood and carnage.

Towards sunset, our picquets were sent down the hill, and I plainly saw them posted among the corpses of those who had fallen in the morning. Nothing, however, immediately near us, presented the idea of recent slaughter; for the loss, on our side, was so partial, and considering the extent of our line, so trifling, that there was little, if any, vestige of it; not so the enemy's; but as they suffered principally on their retreat down the hill, their slain lay towards the bottom of it; from whence, indeed, they had been removing their wounded.

The view of the enemy's camp by night far exceeded, in grandeur, its imposing aspect by day. Innumerable and brilliant fires illuminated all the country spread below us: while they yet flamed brightly, the shadowy figures of men and horses, and the glittering piles of arms, were all visible. Here and there, indeed, the view was interrupted by a few dark patches of black fir, which, by a gloomy contrast, heightened the effect of the picture: but, long after the flames expired, the red embers still emitted the most rich and glowing rays, and seemed, like stars, to gem the dark bosom of the earth, conveying the sublime ideas of a firmament spread beneath our feet. It was long before I could tear myself from the contemplation of this scene. Earnestly did I gaze on it; deeply did it impress, me; and my professional life may never, perhaps, again present to me any military spectacle more truly magnificent. Everyone was fully persuaded that the morning would bring with it a general and bloody engagement. Our line was in a constant state of preparation: the men lay, with their accoutrements on, in a regular column of companies, front and rear ranks head to head, and every man's firelock by his side.

As early, as three o'clock we were roused, and stood to arms, at our posts. In a sort of gorge, between two of those rude misshapen ridges of rock which rise on the Sierras, my regiment was stationed, with another battalion. This gorge was considered one of the most vulnerable points of the whole line; and it was thought that the main efforts of the enemy would be directed against it. At about half past four, the picquets sent word that the enemy was getting under arms: the picquets were immediately and silently withdrawn, and one staff-officer remained on the look-out. About five, he came quickly up: and, as he passed the commander of our line, said, "Be prepared, sir; they are certainly coming on. A very heavy column has just advanced to the foot of the position, and you may expect an attack every moment."

My bosom beat quick, very quick; it was possible, that the few minutes of my existence were already numbered. Such a thought, however, though it will, it must, arise, in the first awful moment of expectation, to the mind of him who has never been engaged, is not either dangerous or despicable, and will rather strengthen than stagger the resolution of a manly heart. And now, thought I, as the first note of an enemy's trumpet struck my ear,—now they come: but no; it ceased, that thrilling sound, and proved only a parley, with a flag of truce, to deliver some trifling message. The sun shone forth, but not on a field of blood; the French columns returned to their ground and appeared, throughout the day, to busy themselves in hutting: towards evening some of them were seen moving, and, at midnight, it was ascertained, that they were all in motion, to turn our right. We now immediately broke up, and descending from our formidable position, recrossed the Mondego, and our corps of the army marched on San Miguel. We all naturally felt the deepest disappointment at having thus marched and toiled, without that sweet reward for which youth and ambition always sigh; many months, however, were yet to elapse before the valued privilege of discharging the important, perilous duties of our profession, was yet to be accorded to us. But, as a lesson in the art of war, none, perhaps, was ever more instructive and interesting than this memorable campaign. Our army, inferior both in numbers and composition to that opposed to us, could only hope for success from the prudent measures, and able guidance, of a wise and valiant general.

From the moment that Almeida fell, the dispositions and movements of Wellington excited universal admiration. He availed himself, most ably, of the only advantage which, with an army like ours, it would, perhaps, have been possible to obtain. He, by a most rapid and skilful manoeuvre, threw us into a position at Buzaco, so strong and commanding, as to be alike secure from the artillery, and inaccessible to the cavalry of the enemy. Here, from the lofty ridge of one of their native Sierras, he first showed to the Portuguese levies the array of their formidable invaders; and here he allotted to them the easy task of repulsing, by the side of British soldiers, one of those desperate and hopeless assaults, which his knowledge of the French character encouraged him to expect.

By this master-stroke of military skill and sound policy, the Portuguese were inspired with a confidence in him and in themselves, which never afterwards forsook them. But Lord

Wellington clearly saw, that in playing for so mighty a stake as the political existence of a nation, the fate of the war should never be suffered to depend on the glorious hazards of a battle; as soon therefore, as he found the position of Buzaco no longer tenable, he decided on retiring to lines near Lisbon, which had been long fortifying with care, and there to defend the seat of the government, and the capital of the country. To give effect, however, to this plan of defence, it was necessary, not only that the allied army should retire to the fortified position of Torres Vedras, but that the whole country between it and the frontier, which it was at all probable the enemy might occupy, should be abandoned by all classes of inhabitants, and that every thing which might contribute to the subsistence, or facilitate the progress of their troops, should be carefully removed. My pen altogether fails me,— I feel that no powers of description can convey to the mind of my reader, the afflicting scenes, the cheerless desolation, we daily witnessed on our march from the Mondego to the lines. Wherever we moved, the mandate which enjoined the wretched inhabitants to forsake their homes, and to remove or destroy their little property, had gone before us. The villages were deserted; the churches, retreats so often, yet so vainly confided in, were, empty; the mountain cottages stood open and untenanted; the mills in the valley, but yesterday so busy, were motionless and silent.

CHAPTER 8

The Lines at Torres Vedras

We bivouacked on the 4th of October, near Thomar: the neighbourhood of this place is exceedingly pretty, and the town itself regularly built, and beautifully clean. It had counted, a few days before, a population of nearly 4000; the morning we entered it, a few hundreds only remained, and these were fearfully hurrying their departure.

There was a remarkably fine convent in this town, of the order of Christ, richly endowed, and very superb in its church, buildings, and every thing connected with its establishment. I had no occasion to ask for admission; I followed a group of noisy muleteers, who had chosen it for their night's lodging, and whose mules were already drinking out of the marble fountain, or trampling over the neat garden, round which ran handsome, high-arched, and echoing cloisters,—yesterday responsive only to the pacing of some thoughtful monk, now resounding with the boisterous laughter, and coarse jests of rude, merry, muleteers. In the kitchen, some lay servants of the convent yet lingered, and the table in the refectory was covered with the crumbs of the last meal, which the banished fathers had that morning partaken of. The church, however large, magnificent, and gloomy, still inspired reverence and awe; and the muleteers, who walked thither with me, sunk into silence, and crossed themselves, as they knelt before the high altar, round which lamps, trimmed by some pious hand, were yet burning. The streets through which I hastened back to my home, (for cannot a tent become our home?) had an air of loneliness, quite oppressive to the heart: no one stood on the thresholds,—no face looked from the casements,—not a voice was to be heard.

The flanks of our line of march from this place were literally covered with the flying population of the country. In Portugal, there are, at no time, many facilities for travelling, and these few the exigencies of the army had very greatly diminished. Rich indeed were those in good fortune, as in possession, who still retained a cabriolet and mules for its service. Those who had bullock-cars, asses, or any mode of transporting their families, and property, looked contented and grateful; for, respectable men and delicate women, of the second class, might on every side be seen walking slowly and painfully on foot, encumbered by heavy burthens of clothes, bedding, and food.

We bivouacked near Santarem on the evening of the sixth. Crowds of the inhabitants, who till our arrival were unwilling to believe that the enemy would be suffered to penetrate so far, were now, with a silent and mournful activity, preparing for flight. I walked slowly towards the house where I had been once so hospitably treated: the doors were barred; the casements shut in; the kind-hearted owner had forsaken, it. I climbed the garden wall, and saw beneath it the plants and flowers, of which himself and his good wife had appeared so proud, arranged as he had probably left them not two days before, and bearing evidence of his latest care.

I returned to the camp by a circuitous path, which led across a vineyard. Here the order had suddenly broken in upon and suspended the cheerful labours of the vintage. In one part the vines were yet teeming with fruit; in another, large heaps of grapes gathered, but not carried to the wine-press, lay deadening in the sun, with baskets half-filled near them; and the print of little feet between the vine-rows showed that children had been sharing the light and pleasing toil, which at that happy season employs their parents. On the following morning our columns traversed the city, and, descending into the Lisbon road, continued their route.

Immediately below the town the bank of the river was crowded with fugitives waiting to be transported across, and the most affecting groups of families sat weeping on the ground. I well remember a serious thoughtful-looking man, of about fifty, seated on a horse, and carrying, before him a very aged mother, who had been bedridden for many years, and who lay, upon his arm so helplessly, and with an aspect so pale and withered, that you might have thought the grave had yielded up its dead. Here monks, gentlemen, peasants, and mendicants, were all crowded together: the silent nun and the complaining damsel sat side by side. There was a strange, yet natural, familiarity among them: natural, for it was the offspring of misery. How soon can the arrows of misfortune level the paltry distinctions of this world! Here vanity was stifled, rank forgotten: all was agitation, anxiety, and alarm.

This melancholy picture was forcibly contrasted by the gay and careless security of our cheerful soldiery. For what, let me ask, does the soldier suffer, compared to the wretched inhabitant. whose country is made the theatre of war? The soldier's wants are all provided for: he is fed and clothed; he sleeps, too, in comparative tranquillity; for, wrapt in his watch-cloak, he reposes in a camp, surrounded by arms and comrades, and ever prepared for resistance, which may indeed bring with it death, but a death always honourable, seldom unrevenged. But to see our dwellings burnt, our daughters insulted, and our families driven forth houseless, this is misery, this is the curse of war; and if as men we are roused up to resist and die, our death is aggravated by all the horrors of acute mental suffering and fearful anxiety. Oh! we hardly suspect, until the dreadful moment of separation arrives, how dear is the roof, be it of marble or of straw, which has from infancy been our home. Good God! how much does that one word convey! The chamber in which we have slept, the festive hoard round which we have so often assembled, the garden in which we have strayed, the many little holidays of the heart we have there enjoyed. It is, not the soldier, the mariner, the merchant, or perhaps even the Englishman, with his boosted fireside, who can feel this so fully as the contented and happy residents in less civilized countries, who having little necessity, and little opportunity for travelling, contract no habits of restlessness, and feel not a wish, dream not of a pleasure; beyond the mountain or the vale, on which their eyes first opened. Moreover, the very practices of their religion in the Peninsula, to them appear to sanctify their dwellings; for all their cottages have their little shrines, saints, and crucifixes, which are regarded by the people with the same affectionate reverence, that marked the attachment of the ancient Romans for their household gods.

On the afternoon of the eighth we entered Alhandra, a, small pretty town on the banks of the Tagus, about four leagues from Lisbon. It lay immediately, in front of the right of our celebrated lines, and was occupied as a sort of advanced post by one brigade of our division, during the whole time that the French remained before them. This town too was deserted; and here, to out very great comfort, we were put under cover, for the weather began to be wet, cold, and disagreeable. In this place a most strange though comfortable lodging fell to the lot of myself and my comrade. We took up our quarters in this sacristy of a church. This chamber was lofty, spacious, and gloomy: twelve figures, as large as life, the images of some departed saints, were placed in niches all round the walls; they were habited, too, in the black dresses of some monastic order; and what with the glare of their eyes, the stirring of their robes, and the faint glimmering of our lamp, they seemed almost to live and move, and frown upon us. They could not, however, repress the mirth, frighten away the appetite, or scare the slumbers of men so cheerful, so hungry, and so .tired as we were. Our cloaks, I remember, and some of our blankets, were excessively damp, which might perhaps have made our night's rest somewhat uncomfortable; luckily for us, however, the priests had left the drawers in the sacristy full of their vestments; and with gay and heavy pontificals spread beneath and over us, we slept as sound as any canon in the closes of York or Durham.

The day after we marched in here, a few prisoners, taken in

a cavalry skirmish near Azimbuja, were brought in. They belonged to the French heavy dragoons, and I thought their appearance particularly martial. The brazen helmet, with the lofty crest, black-horse hair, and tiger-skin band, looked very noble; and the thick wiry *moustachios* of the weather-beaten men who bore them, and who were all wounded, well became these warlike *casques*. The head-dress of our own dragoons has since been greatly improved upon the French model; but at the time I speak of, they still wore awkward shapeless hats.

About nine o'clock on the evening of the tenth, as I was turning into my strange bed, we received orders to march immediately for some fortified heights, about a league and a half to the rear and left. The rain in Portugal is almost as heavy as under the tropics, and it fell this night in continued and overwhelming torrents; it was also uncommonly dark, and I think we were about six hours groping our way as many miles. In the small mountain village where we halted, I got into a:little cottage with my company; but the place was so confined, that we could neither lie down nor even sit, and we remained on our feet, crowded together till daylight, when we divided ourselves among the miserable hovels more equally. The posts and batteries in the neighbourhood, with the defence, of which we were charged for three days, were by no means in a perfectly serviceable condition; as in some, no guns were at the time mounted, and in others, the necessary ammunition had not been provided.

I confess, when I revert to this period of the campaign, I am more and more astonished that Massena never attempted to force our position. The French infantry, which was concentrated in front of us at Buzaco, might certainly, without any very prodigious exertion, have reached our lines by the tenth, and on that, or the ensuing day, might have attacked them. I shall ever be of opinion, that if the enemy had determined to sacrifice everything to the grand object of penetrating our line, and marching on Lisbon, they might very possibly have effected their purpose. It is not to be denied that our position was provided with formidable redoubts and batteries; nevertheless it was a very extensive one, and the defence of it would not altogether have depended on the abilities of Wellington, or the bravery of the army. The confusion or misapprehension of any one general as to what he was to provide for and protect, the fear of responsibility, and the absence of discretion in a common brigadier, might have neutralized both the talents of the leader, and the courage of the men, and proved fatal to our hopes.

We should have been more particularly liable to such a misfortune, in the hurry of the two or three first, days, after we entered the lines, and before the grammar of their defence was thoroughly understood by all our generals. A well-conducted assault would have borne with it the character of a *coup de main*, and must have been decided by musketry and the bayonet: Massena, however, delayed for his, artillery, suffered the golden opportunity to escape him; nor did he, when his guns arrived, venture to attack us.

CHAPTER 9

The Pursuit of the French

On the thirteenth my regiment again moved to Bucellas. Near this town ran the second line of defence, and the post being considered highly important, six British battalions were stationed in it in reserve. The whole time that we remained here our line was regularly under arms two hours before break of day every morning; and when the sun appeared above the horizon, we generally manoeuvred for an hour before we were dismissed. For a few days on our first arrival in this quarter, my friend and I pitched our tent in the market-place. Here I took my meals, but slept with my company in a church, in which about two hundred of our men were accommodated. The senior officer had the sacristy, the next a little chamber or recess behind the high altar, and the rest of us made ourselves truly comfortable in the large organ-loft. I used often to lean out of this gallery, and contemplate the strange scene below me. How a sober citizen from St. Paul's churchyard would have stared to see a serjeant of grenadiers writing his reports on the communion table, a fifer lounging at his ease in the pulpit, and practising his favourite quick step, and the men dividing and calling off their rations of raw beef on tombs of polished marble. Such, however, is but too faithful a picture of an everyday occurrence on actual service.

Lisbon, after the first alarm, became as it were intoxicated by a strong feeling of security: there never was a period when this city was more crowded with objects of misery, or when provisions were more extravagantly dear; yet at no time had their theatres been better filled, their societies more gay and brilliant, than when seventy thousand vindictive enemies lay within sixteen miles of the city, panting for the plunder of it. It is but justice to add, that every thing which prudence and humanity could suggest was done by the inhabitants of Lisbon, to alleviate the public misfortune. The port was open to all vessels laden with provisions, the magazines were filled with them, charitable institutions were set on foot, and food was daily distributed to such of the fugitives as were necessitous and helpless, while labour was provided for the others. The police, too, of the city was most active; and whatever secret and treasonable spirit existed among the disaffected, was compelled to remain inactive and harmless. Still, I thought it strange to see such fearless and inconsistent gaiety among people who might, in the course of a few short hours, be placed at the mercy of a conqueror: but the truth is, we are all the creatures of custom, and a very short experience will reconcile us to anything. Hence it is, that the inhabitants of Portici sleep tranquilly under: the burning, Vesuvius, and mariners sing jovially while locked upon the restless waves, in which the starting of a single plank might engulf them for ever!

From a lofty height, about half a league from Bucellas, I could command a view of the Tagus; and here I frequently walked, and distinctly saw the gun-boats stationed on the right of our position, exchanging their fire with the French cannon at Villa Franca. The immediate neighbourhood of Villa Franca is covered with handsome *quintas*, and on some of them I had gazed, on my passage up the Tagus in July 1809, with pardonable envy. How little did my mind, at that time, associate with scenes so smiling, the ideas of devastation and death!

Our army, during the whole of this period, was supplied with provisions from the commissariat stores at Lisbon; and these were conveyed to us at times, in a manner amusingly novel.

I remember well, one day, seeing a file of about one hundred *cabriolets* laden with sacks of biscuit and flour; and the evening's amusement of many a fair lady was, by the absence of her carriage on this coarse, but useful service, altogether destroyed. While we remained in this cantonment, a Portuguese officer died, in the town; I attended the funeral, and was very much impressed with the ceremony. The custom of exposing the body, dressed as in life and health, on an open bier, may, by its frequency, produce little effect on the natives of Portugal; but to the eye of an Englishman it carries with it an air of solemnity, painful yet salutary; and I defy him to look upon the pale features of a clay-cold corpse with the same light-hearted indifference, that he too often regards the passing hearse in England.

I have more than once distinctly stated, that it is not my intention to offer a professional view of the progress and conduct of the war, or to enter at all upon a regular detail of movements and positions. My humble wish is to draw a picture of campaigning: and if I succeed in recalling one scene of interest to the mind of any veteran who served in the Peninsula, or if I kindle one spark of enthusiasm in the bosom of a youthful soldier, however feebly I may have written, I feel that I shall not have written in vain, I have deemed it necessary to repeat this, that it may not be supposed that a man, with any knowledge of, or attachment to his profession, could be inattentive to the relative situations of the opposing armies, so extraordinary at the period of which I write, and on which it might be expected I should comment and enlarge. No; such a task would far exceed the limits of a light trifling work like this, and would, moreover, be presumptuous in an officer of my age and rank. I consider the Peninsula war to have been a most instructive course of military study; and I have, in common with other officers, treasured up the lessons it afforded with care, and the hope of future advantage.

On the night of the 14th of November, the enemy retired from the position they had so long occupied in our front; and on the 15th, about midday, our column moved from Bucellas: we marched six leagues, passing through Alhandra, Villa Franca, and Villa Nova, and halted at Caregada. The day was wet and stormy, and the roads deep and heavy; but our line of march was all gaiety and animation. To follow up a retreating army is at all times amusing; but when you do so for the first time, your curiosity and pleasure are almost puerile.

On approaching Villa Franca, our eyes were all busily engaged in marking the traces of the French. Here, to the left, was a path worn by their sentries; here, again, had lain the main body of their picquet: there, to the right, they had planted two guns; instead of sand-bags or gabions, several large painted garden tubs, with the plants that once adorned them cut away, had been piled up to form a battery. At the entrance of Villa Franca, the street was barricaded; chests, wine-casks, and mattresses, formed the strange barrier: here, on one of the very first houses, a chalk scribble showed it had been the quarter of a company of French grenadiers; there had been the billet of a *chef de bataillon;* in that neat looking mansion with green window shutters and unbroken windows, had lodged, as appeared by a scribble over the door, a *chef d'état major.* In short, look where you would, you saw spots that were yesterday peopled with your enemies; men wearing a different dress, speakings different language, and ready to fight and bleed in a different cause.

It was late in the evening when we arrived at Caregada, and the town was already filled with our troops, principally artillery and cavalry. The houses and stables; were all occupied; and into these last, some of our officers and men, with great difficulty, got admission. By far the greater proportion of us, however, passed this dark and dreary night in the open streets. In a town which had been for weeks deserted by its inhabitants, and so lately evacuated:by an enemy, as may readily be supposed, there was no want of dry fuel, and we made large fires, without being very scrupulous in our choice of wood; old planks, palings, doors, and window-shutters, were consumed with very little hesitation. Many of us sent to borrow chairs from those houses already occupied, and sat lounging round our fires till daybreak. The scene was altogether diverting: we had no cooking, for the baggage was not up, and there was of course nothing to be had in an empty town: a little biscuit, and a draught of country wine from a soldier's wooden canteen, was my supper; and I leaned back in a chair my corporal had got for me, all cushioned with blue damask, and ornamented with gilding, and attempted, but in vain, to sleep. The continued rain kept my shoulders wet and chilly, while the blazing fire scorched my legs, so that it was impossible to preserve the same posture for five minutes.

At length day came; the cavalry and artillery moved, and in a few minutes I thought myself highly fortunate to get into a room with four others: a room which had once, perhaps, been handsome and comfortable; but had then neither furniture, doors, or casements.

After enjoying the luxury of a basin of hot tea, I visited a small camp, which had been constructed by the enemy, near the town; for two brigades of French infantry had been hutted in the immediate vicinity. These huts were exceedingly neat, well-built, and arranged in a regular line, with a fine piece of ground well-cleared to the front. The huts of the officers were large, and very commodious, having many little ingenious contrivances for comfort and convenience. I was much struck by one thing I observed here, and which, no doubt, a good catholic would have considered as a most daring and impious profanation: a French officer had torn out a large scripture painting, which had been the altar-piece of some chapel, and had spread it, with the subject outwards, over his hut, and here he had lain, sheltered from the rain by canvass, which the representation of some holy scene, or miraculous event, had rendered sacred in the eyes of the people, and before which many a knee had been bent, and many a head bowed in reverence, for the space, perhaps; of a century before. In one small neat little bower, I found lying on the ground a small Paris edition of *St Pierre's Studies of Nature*; it had apparently been much read, and had probably charmed and consoled the solitary hours of some amiable man, whom attachment to the profession of arms had led to march under the eagles of Napoleon. Yes, in the French army, as in all others, the good hearts far outnumber the bad; much that we hear of the ferocity and cruelties of armies is untrue; much exaggerated. It is true, that soldiers (I shall speak not of officers) have a blameable disposition to waste and destroy; but it is the heedless and mischievous wantonness of the schoolboy, not the vindictive malice of the man.

Soldiers are often placed in situations, which, from their nature and their novelty, give birth to an elevation of spirits it is difficult to control. I have seen common men distributed through a suite of rooms in the empty palace of a nobleman: they have been surrounded by mirrors and marble, and I have observed in their countenances a jocular eagerness to smash and destroy them. But this does not arise out of cruelty. No: in such a case, a soldier feels himself lifted, for a moment, above his low and ordinary condition; while the banished owner of the proud mansion, in which he lodges, appears humbled below him; and that mind must be superior to human infirmity, which did not, at such a thought, carelessly exult. But I am persuaded that the sudden appearance of the sufferer, and his weeping family, in ninety-nine cases out of a hundred, would reproduce the generous feelings of pity and forbearance. Again, on the subject of plunder, setting aside assaults or battles, the soldier is often harassed with toil and hunger, impatient and penniless. It is the object and the end of discipline to prevent and punish plunder under circumstances like these; for it is seldom in any other that a soldier, in any army, (even a French one,) turns marauder. But when troops are neither fed, clothed or paid with regularity, they are tempted beyond their strength; and the military man, who has served, learns how and when to make allowances for those disorders, which the world is ever too forward to characterise as barbarous and licentious. My opinion of the moral excellence of soldiers is very superior to that generally entertained; and I think that we should find as much virtue, and as many amiable qualities, among ten thousand soldiers, as among a similar number of individuals taken, without selection, from the bosom of civil society.

It will be remarked by those who live among soldiers, that they are charitable and generous, kind to children, and fond of dumb animals: add to this, a, frequent exposure to hardship, privation and danger, makes them friendly, and ready to assist each other. Nor are they without a just and laudable pride. The worthless characters who are to be met with in every regiment (and society) are generally shunned; nor have I ever seen an expression of discontent on their countenances at the just punishment of a moral offender.

We marched forwards the next morning to Azimbuja; here we learned that the enemy had taken up a position at Santarem, that Lord Wellington had halted at Cartaxo, and that our force, under Hill, was to cross immediately to the south bank of the Tagus. About four hundred French prisoners, taken in front, passed through this place for Lisbon. They were all infantry, for the most part weak and sickly stragglers, and a few incautious marauders; these last alone retained the appearance of soldiers. The French foot usually march and fight in their great coats; a practice certainly convenient and economical, but carrying with it a very dull and dirty appearance. Their cap, however, is always soldier-like and handsome, and when they do wear their full uniform, I think the general effect good The red worsted epaulettes give breadth to the shoulders; and the coat, with the facings buttoned back, and the skirts sloped away above the hips, give lightness and height to the whole figure.

In Azimbuja I had a pretty little chamber, with doors, windows, and some little furniture preserved, probably by the *chef d'escadron*, who had lodged here before me, and who had left behind him, in a favourite quotation, which I found scribbled everywhere on the walls, a pretty faithful sample of his spirit: "*Le premier, qui fut Roi, fut un soldat heureux*"

On the 19th we were transported across the Tagus by the boats of the fleet, which had been sent up the river, with a proportion of officers and seamen for that purpose. Admiral Sir Thomas Williams and Captain Beresford superintended the passage of the troops; and this important service was performed for us by the navy with their accustomed order, expedition, and regularity. From this period, until the latter end of February, we were stationed at Almeyrim, a small country town, about two miles from the left bank of the Tagus, and directly opposite Santarem, the headquarters of the French army. Almeyrim would, in itself, have been insupportably dull, as there were no families in the place above the middling class in life, and the scenery around was not remarkable for its beauty; but from the relative position of the armies, it proved exceedingly interesting: for, although we remained nearly three months unmolested by the enemy, and inactive ourselves, we could none of us feel certain that we should continue so. We should never have been surprised, had the alarm drum, at midnight, roused us from our beds; and the idea that this was possible, took from the insipidity of a life, in other respects, monotonous. Our picquets lay on the bank of the river, and could plainly observe, with the naked eye, every motion of, the enemy in the lower town of Santarem, and on the roads which led out from the, city. On that leading to Cartaxo, we every day saw their picquets posted, and their fatigue parties felling trees to form abatis, digging entrenchments, or constructing breast-works; while; on that to their rear, forage-parties, detachments, or orderlies; were constantly going out and returning.

All this was to me an inexhaustible source of amusement; I often walked out with my glass, and passed whole mornings in watching them: here I would see a troop of their dragoons exercising on the plain below the town; there a general officer riding out with his staff; here some field-officer visiting his guards and picquets; and there several of their men washing and cleaning their arms and appointments on the very brink of the stream. You constantly heard the sound of their voices; and, on a still day, might readily distinguish what they said. We often, indeed, conversed courteously with their officers; until the prating impudence of some individual caused such intercourse to be forbidden, most properly, I admit; for simplicity and indiscretion might have produced incalculable mischief.

About a mile from Almeyrim, embosomed among trees, but commanding a fine view of the towers and buildings of Upper

Santarem, stood a beautiful *quinta*, in his happier and innocent days, the residence of the Marquis de Alorna, a nobleman of Portugal, once a general in her armies; but one who, deceived or corrupted by the French, had fled his country, openly espoused their cause, and had now returned as the guide and counsellor of their legions. This miserable man was, for three months, resident in Santarem; a town in which he had often, no doubt, been greeted with affection and respect, by a smiling and a happy population; but where his eye now encountered, on every side, the glance of suspicion, contempt, or indignation from foreigners, who, notwithstanding their own bold and lawless aggressions, may sometimes reverence the patriot who opposes them, but will ever distrust and despise the very traitor who serves them. The *quinta de Alorna* was at this time occupied by some servants, who held it for the crown; and many a morning did I pass there, reading in the library, walking on the terrace, and wandering in the grounds. I learned, from some of the peasants, that the marquis had been a kind landlord, a tender husband and father, and had passed many months every year in this pleasing retreat. What must such a man have felt, when, from the window of his cheerless billet, he looked down upon this family mansion, and knew that he was banished from it for ever! I can hardly image to myself a situation more painful:—he must have regarded the *quinta* as a fearful monument of days of peace, gone by for ever; as the tomb of his honour and happiness, the grave of all his hopes

Of all criminals, I look upon the traitor as one, whose punishment in this life is the most certain; for it is a punishment which the smiles of fortune and of power can neither avert or soften: it is a restless poison of the mind, an ever-aching void in the desolate and lonely heart:—kindred, friendship, love, all cast from their blessed bosoms the wretch who has betrayed his country.

About the middle of February, as I was one day walking by the river side with three or four companions, we observed an unusual crowd on the opposite bank, and several French officers. They saluted us with a "*Bon jour, Messieurs*" and soon we fell into conversation. They were exceedingly courteous. They spoke in the highest terms of Romana, who had lately died, calling him "*Le seul général Espagnol digne de son grade.*"

They asked after Lord Wellington; saying he had done wonders with the Portuguese, and praising him greatly for his conduct of the campaign. They next enquired, if our king was not dead; and on our replying that he was not, one of them spoke, but inaudibly; another, in a louder voice, repeated "*Le général dit, que tout le monde aime votre Roi George, qu'il a été bon père de famille, et bon père de son peuple.*"

We were thus, at once, let into the rank of one of their party, and not a little delighted at the manner in which they had spoken of our excellent and unfortunate sovereign. A great deal of good humour prevailed; we quizzed each other freely. They asked us how we liked *bacallâo* and *azete*, instead of English roast beef: and we, what they did at Santarem without the restaurateurs, cafés, and *salles de spectacle* of their dear Paris? They replied, laughing, that they had a theatre; and asked us to come over, and witness the performance of that evening, which would be, "*L'Entrée des François dans Lisbon.*"

A friend of mine most readily replied, that he recommended to them "*La répétition d'une nouvelle piéce, 'La Fuite des François.'*" They burst into a long, loud, and general laugh:—the joke was too good, too home. Their general, however, did not think it wise to remain longer; but he pulled off his hat, and wishing us good day with perfect good humour, went up the hill, and the group immediately dispersed.

CHAPTER 10

Albuera

On the 21st of February some alarm was excited by a party of the enemy crossing over to a large island in the Tagus, about a league above Santarem, and immediately opposite Alpiaça, a small town on the south bank. They, however, only foraged it, and retired, without attempting to establish any communication with Alemtejo; but we, in consequence, fixed a post on the island, to secure it against further insult. I was one of the party stationed here from the 1st to the 5th of March. A loop-holed chapel, a circular pigsty, dignified with the name of a redoubt, and a few miserable hovels, formed the defences and cantonments of our little garrison, which consisted of two companies of infantry and twelve dragoons. On the night of the fourth of March, as I was going my rounds, my ear caught some unusual noise on the French bank; and approaching to the edge of the water, and lying down, I distinctly heard the trampling of horses, the sound of wheels, and the cracking of whips. For three hours I lay perfectly still, listening to those truly grateful sounds. It was now evident that a second campaign was about to open; and that we should leave the narrow limits we had occupied since October, for some new and more interesting scenes. The next day our detachment quitted the island and it was known that the enemy had broke up from Santarem, and was in full retreat

On the sixth, about noon, we marched from Alpiaça, in the highest possible spirits. After moving for four days through a very pretty country, our brigade was halted in a small neat village of

Alemtejo, about one league from Abrantes. I had forgot to mention, that the command of all the troops on the south bank of the Tagus had, in the absence of General Hill, who was ordered home for the recovery of his health, been entrusted to Marshal Beresford. This officer had, by the direction of Lord Wellington, taken with him a considerable detachment of his army corps, and pursued the retreating divisions of Massena, in the direction of Thomar; where, it was inferred from his first movements, he had some intention of collecting a force. The French commander, however, proceeded for the Mondego, and was followed by the main body of the allies, headed by Wellington in person. The proposed operations of our little army, in Spanish Estremadura, were, from these dispositions, of necessity suspended, until the return of the Marshal and his detachment During this short interval we remained stationary in our quiet cantonment The cottages in which we were quartered were pleasingly scattered over the face of the country had all their little gardens, in the midst of which they stood, and their walls, clothed with the creeping vine, which extended itself over their humble roofs, or spreading along a sort of light trellis-work, formed grateful and shady porticoes before their doors.

The season of the year, too, was warm and delightful as an English May. Some orange groves in the neighbourhood were in high beauty, and presented us with a sight altogether novel. The same tree, from which you pluck the ripe and juicy, orange, presents you, on the neighbouring branch, the delicate blossom, and again, on another, the unripe fruit, green and flavourless. There were, the most beautiful walks and rides in every direction around us, and nothing could be more rural than the scene constantly before our eyes. Nor was the pleasure at all diminished by seeing two distinct classes of society, very strongly contrasted: to observe, on the same spot, the peaceful demeanour of husbandmen, and the tumultuous gaiety of soldiers; to hear the tinkling guitar, silenced by drums, trumpets, and bugles, sounding the hour of rest; to see the rustics going quietly forth at sunrise, to their daily labour, and the soldiers coming, fully armed, from vine-covered cottages, and hurrying with brisk steps to the field of exercise; to mark the gay confidence of our men, and the silent humility, yet eager wonder of the peasants. All this gave a man something to think of in his walks, which made him forget the want of a book, or a companion. The soldiers, too, seemed to feel all the ordinary delight which such a scene, in the soft season of spring, naturally inspires, even in uncultivated minds, and they were all health and high spirits.

On the eighteenth of the month we were again in motion, and marched, by Portalegre, to Arronches, where we rested three days. When Massena broke up from Santarem on the fifth, we, on the south bank, had calculated on marching to the relief of Badajos, an important fortress; in Spanish Estremadura, at that time besieged by the Duke of Dalmatia. This design, with the execution of which we should certainly have been charged, was frustrated by the governor, who suddenly surrendered the place to a weak corps of the enemy, on terms the most disgraceful. The fall of Badajos was immediately followed by the attack and capture of Campo Mayor; a place not capable of any resistance, and from which, indeed, we ourselves drove the enemy, two days after they had entered it.

It was on the afternoon of the twenty-fifth that we halted in a very pretty bivouack, on the banks of the Caya: our camp lay in a beautiful valley surrounded by hills; on the sides of these the infantry took up their ground, while our cavalry occupied the verdant flat of the banks of the stream.

On the morning of the twenty-sixth we marched upon Campo Mayor: and, at the distance of about two miles from its walls, we halted to let the cavalry pass to the front They were about 2000 in number; they moved past us in file at a brisk trot; their cattle were in beautiful condition, and occasionally broke into a proud prancing canter.

It is at such a moment, and in such a situation, that an infantry officer cannot altogether suppress a feeling of envy. It is true, that to his service belongs the tug of war, and that more men are killed in one hour by a hot fire of musketry, than in one day of galloping and sabring; for the injury of a sabre-cut, as compared to a gunshot wound, is, in nine cases out of ten, trifling; still the heart will follow the trampling of a squadron of cavalry, the rattling of all their appointments, and the noble animating sound of their brazen trumpets. On this particular day I felt this very strongly: we knew that there was every probability of a handsome affair with the enemy, who would of course, evacuate the town, and retire upon Badajos; but the nature of the ground was so favourable for the operations of horse, that it. was also very likely the engagement would be entirely confined to troops of that arm. Our suspicions were not ill-founded; the French were no sooner apprised of our advance, then they hastily formed behind the town. Four regiments of their cavalry presented a front to our people, while their infantry (a column of about 1200) commenced its retreat, carrying with it several pieces of artillery.

A most brilliant charge was made upon the enemy's dragoons by our Thirteenth Light, supported by the Portuguese. Our people behaved with great intrepidity; but the affair was altogether conducted, on our part, with such a total absence of skill, that the French secured the retreat of their infantry and guns, sustaining indeed a loss[11], but a loss very little heavier than our own. Our fine brigade of heavy cavalry was never brought up to the enemy, and our columns of infantry followed slowly in the rear. At every half mile we met some mark of this ill-conducted contest, which was carried on to the very gates of Badajos; near which, several of our men, who, consulting only their courage, had pursued without any order or regularity, and, indeed, with the main body of the French cavalry marching on in their rear, were captured. In spite of the interest excited on such a day, it is mortifying to a man of spirit, and painful to a man of feeling, to follow, in cold blood, and gaze upon the piteous spectacle of dead and dying, scattered in your path. I remember well, among the events of this day, having remarked one fine manly corpse very particularly; it lay a few yards from the road-side, alone, na-

---

11. About 300 killed, wounded, and taken.

ked, the face and breast downwards, and on the back of the head a deep and frightful cleft, inflicted by the sabre; all round the spot where it lay the ground was deeply indented with the print of horses' feet, who appeared to have gone over it at a furious pace. The sky was cloudy, and the wind high; the body was cold, and pale, the fine formed limbs stiff and motionless; the spirit, which had animated it, not an hour before, had indeed fled: yet I know not how it was; the very corpse made a forcible appeal to the feelings, and seemed to suffer, it looked so comfortless, so humbled, so deserted.

An English dragoon, leading a wounded horse, and conducting two prisoners, one of whom had sabre-cuts on the cheek and shoulder, passed me while I was contemplating this scene. "Do you recollect," said I, "friend, what took place here?"

"Yes, sir; they shewed us a front here, and we charged and drove them; but this man, who was an officer, tried to rally them, and was cut down by our adjutant, as I think."

At this moment, one of the French horsemen, leaning down, exclaimed, "*C'est le colonel.*" "*Comment diable,*" said the other.

"*C'est bien lui,*" said his comrade; "*il est mort. Ah! qu'il étoit brave soldat, ce vilain champ de bataille n'est pas digne d'un tel victime.*"

They passed on. What! this carcass, on which the flies were already settling, which lay, all spurned and bloodstained, on the rude and prickly heath, had been, but one short hour before, a man of rank, perhaps also of talent, fortune, courage, whose voice breathed command, whose eye glanced fire, whose arm shook defiance;—even so, such is war!

The same day a young French officer was taken by the falling of his horse; he was of the *compagnie d'élite* of the Twenty-Sixth Dragoons; a handsome youth, with a fine fair complexion; a serjeant escorted him past our column, which was, at the time, halted. I shall never forget the mortified and mournful dejection of his countenance: he suffered the bridle of his horse to hang on its neck, and sat in the saddle, thoughtfully careless. As he passed us, some of our officers moved their hats to him; he returned their salute, taking off his large bearskin cap with much grace, but I could see that his eyes were filled with tears. A very few yards behind us, he had to pass a Portuguese column, whose officers crowded forward to look at him, with a sort of triumphant curiosity; though his back was to me, I saw that this awakened all his pride and spirit, for he placed himself erect in his seat, spurred and reined up his horse, and rode slowly and haughtily by them.

Two days after the affair, a flag of truce came to Elvas, to bring this young man some baggage and money. The French captain who came, remained with his young friend for half an hour, in the officers' guard room, at one of the barriers. The trumpeter, who accompanied the flag, was a *vieux* moustache, of about forty, with the chevrons of twenty years' service on his arm. This man, when the two friends came out, and the captain mounted, rode up to the young officer, and cordially grasping his hand, put into it a purse of money, and rode off. The purse, I found, had been made up among the privates of the *compagnie d'élite*, who had charged the old trumpeter with its delivery. This was too strong a testimony, both of the amiability and gallantry of this youth, not to create a deep feeling of interest for him; and it was sorrowful to think, that he might be doomed for years, perhaps, to pine away, in an obscure garret at some depôt of prisoners in England; his professional hopes and prospects blasted, and the brightest season of his life chilled by poverty, and consumed in inaction. But, to return.—After being in motion the whole day, alternately amused by the sight of prisoners and captured horses, and our own dragoons displaying the curious contents of the valises they had plundered, and, again, shocked by the sight of slain and wounded, we retraced our steps to Campo Mayor, and encamped close to its walls.

The next day we marched to Elvas, where we halted till the first of April, when we moved to Borba, a very pretty town, about six leagues from Elvas, and highly celebrated for its rich and excellent wine. While we were thus disposed of in cantonments, our engineers were busily employed in throwing a bridge over the Guadiana at Jurumenha. This work proceeded but slowly, from the great want of materials, and was rendered extremely difficult, front the heavy and sudden rises of the river, caused by the melting of the snows. A flying bridge was, however, at length established, and our army was transported to the Spanish bank in safety, and without opposition, on the night of the fifth of April. On the sixth we moved about three miles, and took up our ground on a plain covered with gumcistus; a small village, lying a little to the rear of our right, was occupied by the headquarters and staff. Here a most extraordinary accident occurred, for which it is difficult to account satisfactorily. A body of the enemy eluded the vigilance of some Portuguese outposts, and surprised a squadron of English dragoons, all of whom they captured. These dragoons had been, for twenty-four hours previous, on out-line piquet, and were desired to consider themselves released from duty, though they were still kept close to the line of piquets; an arrangement by which, combined with the utter want of caution in the outposts, they were taken. But this was not all: the enemy arrived at Marshal Beresford's quarter in the village, and the first alarm was given by the fire of a serjeant's guard, posted over the person of the marshal. They took several horses belonging to the staff from their stables; and if they had not been unnecessarily alarmed, to find that they had penetrated so far, they might have carried off the whole of our headquarter staff, for they returned themselves unmolested.

On the morning of the eighth we moved to invest Olivença, in which the enemy had shut up a small garrison. The occupation of this place was absolutely necessary to us as a depôt, or *place d'armes*; for the French had a very strong garrison in Badajos, which might avail itself of our march to the front, to insult, or altogether interrupt, our communications; and, for the same reason, we constructed a *tête du pont* at Jurumenha.

The order of our march, on the morning of the eighth, was very beautiful. We moved in four parallel columns, at well regulated intervals. The two flank columns were of cavalry, who marched with advanced guards and flankers; the two central columns were divisions of infantry, with their guns. The skirmishers of the 13th Dragoons moved on some eminences to the left of our line of march, and kept an eager lookout on the Badajos road; while the advanced guard of the heavy cavalry, on the right, pursued one of the roads which led directly on the town of Olivença, our near approach to which was announced by the sound of its cannon. From the nature of the country we passed over, all the columns had a fine distinct view of each other, and we all came in sight of the fortress nearly at the same moment; and halting on the heights which overlooked it, just out of gunshot, had a full view of the place while the summons went in.

On a day like this, every one seems on the *qui vive*. All faces are cheerful, all eyes strained; spy-glasses are out; and every one looks pleased who has been lucky enough to distinguish a brazen helmet, a broad-topped cap, or, in fact, any thing French. The governor rejecting the summons, General Cole was left with the fourth division to conduct the siege, and on the afternoon of the tenth the army advanced. I was on the rear guards and as the main body moved two hours before us, it was already dark when we reached the bivouack. There was a something so strikingly beautiful in the appearance of it, that I shall never forget the picture. The night was excessively dark, and, under such, circumstances, the common camp fires would of themselves have produced a fine effect; but, they had been for the most part made in hollow cork-trees, of which great numbers were scattered through the ground; and to see the red fires in their fantastic cavities, and the bright, and consuming flames issuing from their tops, illuminating the pale branches, causing a red atmosphere above, and showing to great advantage the troops, their arms and horses, was a scene so picturesque, so magical, that no description could do it justice.

Olivença, which was only, provided with a garrison of four hundred men, fell as soon as ever it was possible to bring guns to bear on it, and was occupied by the division which besieged it: the rest of us pushed many leagues southward. At Los Santos de Maimona, another affair took place between our cavalry and a small body of the enemy's horse. Our people killed and wounded several, and took about seventy prisoners; but were certainly not successful, to the extent we might have been, had they been more vigorously pushed. These prisoners were hussars, very handsomely clothed and appointed, particularly those of the tenth French. This corps wore a jacket and *pelisse* of light blue or French grey, neatly ornamented with white lace and black fur: their caps, boots,, and accoutrements, excellent: their hair clubbed in a .manner not unbecoming; and their whole appearance soldier-like.

We lay for a few days at Zafra, a clean good city, on the route to Andalusia. We looked forward with eager hope to the chance of a triumphant march over the Sierra Morena, that rude and majestic barrier of southern Spain. The towers of fair Seville already seemed to rise before us; and, in. imagination, we were already wandering amid the romantic scenery on the banks of the far-famed Guadalquiver. Badajos, however, was first to be gained; a fortress, the possession of which was to us most important, whether we looked to offensive operations in Spain, or to the mere defence of Portugal.

We broke up from our cantonments on the third of May: the same evening our division arrived at Talavera-Real, a town on the high road to Badajos, and distant from it about ten miles. It was just at the dawn of day, on the fourth, that the heads of all the columns, destined to besiege Badajos, crowned every little eminence round the city, and formed the investment of the place. Our previous night-march had been well arranged as to time; and this operation, which is at all times interesting, was executed, on this occasion, with admirably skill, and in the most beautiful order. The sky was cloudless and serene, the morning air mild and pleasant. The enemy's picquets skirmished prettily with our advance, and they threw both shot and shells from the town, but with little or no effect. They sent out the few dragoons they had, to assist in reconnoitering our force; and these men performed their duty, with a degree of coolness and intrepidity, which could not have been surpassed. I saw individuals ride up within pistol-shot of our infantry skirmishers; and one man galloped boldly as near to a column, not very distant from the height on which my regiment was formed. The scene was quite a review one: the walls of Badajos were crowded with spectators; and from the top of the castle the tricoloured standard, an ensign which has spread terror over half Europe, was calmly floating. Our regiment lay for four days in a small narrow dell, under cover of their fire, but within gun-shot of the city.

On the night of the eighth, our brigade broke ground; at so considerable a distance, however, that we sustained no loss, but opened the first parallel, and covered ourselves before break of day. I regard the operations of a siege highly interesting; the daily progress of the labours; the trenches filled with men, who lie secure within range of the garrison; the fire of the batteries; the beautiful appearance of the shells and fire-balls by night; the challenges of the enemy's sentries; the sound of their drums and trumpets; all give a continued charm and animation to this service. But the duties of a besieging force are both harassing and severe; and, I know not how it is, death in the trenches never carries with it that stamp of glory, which seals the memory of those, who perish in a well-fought field. The daily exploits of the northern army under Lord Wellington, and Graham's victory at Barossa, made us restless and mortified at our comparative ill fortune; for as yet we had struggled only with privation, hardship, and disease.

On, the 13th, in the afternoon, while lounging in our camp of ease, about four miles from the trenches, we were surprised by an order, to hold ourselves in readiness to march, at the shortest notice. Reports soon began to circulate, that Soult was moving rapidly, at the head of a considerable force, to succour Badajos; that a corps of Spaniards, under the orders of Blake, was marching from Ayamonte, to co-operate with us; that the siege was to be immediately raised; and that a battle might be shortly expected. On the 14th we broke up, and marched upon Valverde; halted for the night, and moved forwards at midday, on the 15th, to Albuera, which place we reached about five in the evening. Our cavalry had already retired upon this post; the enemy's horse, who were vastly superior. in number, having pushed them from Santa Martha in the morning. Albuera, the scene of a most murderous and sanguinary conflict, it may not be amiss to describe. It is a small inconsiderable village, uninhabited, and in ruins: it is situated on a stream from which it takes its name, and over which there are two bridges; one about two hundred yards to the right of the village, large, handsome, and built of hewn stone; the other, close to the left of it, small, narrow, and incommodious. This brook is not above knee-deep: its banks, to the left of the small bridge, are abrupt and uneven; and, on that side, both artillery and cavalry would find it difficult to pass, if not impossible; but to the right of the main bridge, it is accessible to any description of force. The enemy occupied a very large extensive wood, about three quarters of a mile distant, on the other side of the stream, and posted their picquets close to us. The space between the wood and the brook was a level plain; but on our side the ground rose considerably, though there was nothing which could be called a height, as from Albuera to Valverde[12] every inch of ground is favourable to the operations of cavalry—not a tree, not a ravine, to interrupt their movements.

I shall here interrupt my private recollections, to give a rapid and general sketch of the battle, which took place on the morrow. On the morning of the 16th our people were disposed as follows: The Spanish army[13], under the orders of General Blake, was on the right, in two lines, its left rested on the Valverde road on which, just at the ridge of an ascent, rising from the main bridge, the right of our division (the second) was posted, the left of it extending to the Badajos road, on ground elevated above the village, which was occupied by two battalions of German riflemen; General Hamilton's Portuguese division being on the left of the whole. General Cole, with

---

12. I consider the wood, near Valverde, as too distant from the scene of action at Albuera to be considered, in any way, when speaking generally of the face of the country.
13. It joined us on the night of the 15th.

two brigades of the fourth division (the fusilier brigade and one of Portuguese), arrived a very short time before the action, and formed, with them, our second line. These dispositions the enemy soon compelled us to alter.

At eight o'clock he began to move; and menacing, with two columns, the village and bridges. under cover of his cavalry, he filed the main body of his infantry over the rivulet, beyond our right, and attacked that flank with very superior numbers and with great impetuosity. The greater part of the Spaniards hastily formed front to the right to meet the attack; and, after a short and gallant resistance, were overpowered and driven from their ground. The enemy now commanded and raked our whole position: the fire of his artillery was heavy, but fortunately for us, not very well directed. It became now imperiously necessary to retake, at any price, the important post, unfortunately, not blameably, lost by the Spaniards. The three brigades of the division Stewart marched on it in double quick time, led by that general. The first, or right brigade, commanded by Colonel Colborne, was precipitated into action under circumstances the most unfavourable: it deployed by corps as it arrived near the enemy, fired, and was in the act of gallantly charging with the bayonet on the heavy column of their infantry, when a body of Polish lancers, having galloped round upon its rear in this most unfortunate moment (for a charge is often a movement of exulting confusion), overthrew it with a great and cruel slaughter. The 31st Regiment, not having deployed, escaped this misfortune; and the third brigade, under General Houghton, and second, under Colonel Abercromby, successively arriving re-established the battle, and, with the assistance of the fusilier brigade under Sir William Myers, the fortunes of this bloody day were retrieved, and the French driven in every direction from the field. I should not omit to mention, that, during the whole of the day, there was very heavy skirmishing near the village, which was occupied and held, throughout the contest, by the German light infantry, under the orders of Major-General Alten. General Lumley, who commanded the allied cavalry, displayed great ability, and foiled every attempt of the enemy's horse to turn our right[14], who were in that arm very superior, and who directed their efforts repeatedly to that object The Portuguese troops, with the exception of one brigade, were very little engaged in this affair, and numbers of the Spanish troops never came into action. The brunt of the battle fell on the British, who lost 4,103 killed and wounded, including in this number 120 of the German Legion. The Portuguese lost about 400; the Spaniards 1,800: making a total of about 6,300. The French lost, at the lowest calculation, 9,000. Soult had about 24,000; and we were, perhaps, in point of numbers, a little superior to him altogether, but had only 7,000 English.

The two British brigades, who more particularly distinguished themselves on this glorious day, were the fusilier brigade, commanded and led by Sir William Myers, and the third brigade of the second division, headed by General Houghton. The first of these, composed of two battalions of the 7th Regiment and one of the 23rd, lost upwards of 1,000 men; and the other, composed of the 29th, first 48th, and 57th Regiments, lost 1,050 men killed and wounded, having entered the field about 1,400 strong. This last brigade went into action led by a major-general, and with its due proportion of field-officers and captains. I saw it at three in the afternoon:—a captain commanded the brigade; the 57th and 48th Regiments were commanded by lieutenants; and the junior captain of the 29th Regiment was the senior effective officer of his corps. Not one of these six regiments lost a man by the sabre or the lance; they were never driven, never thrown into confusion; they fought in line, sustaining and replying to a heavy fire, and often charging; and when the enemy at length fled, the standards of these heroic battalions flew in proud, though mournful triumph, in the centre of their weakened but victorious lines.

I have read the annals of modern warfare with some attention,

14. This may sound inconsistent; but it will be understood that the order of battle was changed from its commencement; and again, the Polish Horse were but a small body, detached for a particular object.

and I know of little which can compare with, nothing which has surpassed, the enthusiastic and unyielding bravery, displayed by these corps on the field of Albuera. Yet this dear-bought, and, let me add, not useless victory, won by unaided courage, graced with no trophies, and followed by no proportionate result, has almost sunk into oblivion, or is remembered only, and spoken of, as a day of doubtful success, if not of positive disaster. It was certainly not useless, because the object of Marshal Soult, which was the relief of Badajos, and the expulsion of our troops from Spanish Estremadura, was wholly defeated; but it had yet a higher, a nobler, a more undying use, it added one to the many bright examples of British heroism; it gave a terrible and long-remembered lesson to the haughty legions of France; and, when Soult rode by the side of his Imperial master on the field of Waterloo, as the cheering of the English soldiery struck upon his ear, Albuera was not forgotten, and he could have whispered him, that they were men, who could only be defeated, by being utterly destroyed.

So much for the battle, generally considered. I would now relate what fell under my own observation, and describe, if it be possible, my feelings on that day. We stood to our arms an hour before break of day: it was a brilliant sight, at sunrise, to see the whole of the French cavalry moving on the plain; but in a short time they retired into the wood, leaving their piquets as before. The battalion being dismissed, I breakfasted, and immediately afterwards set out to walk towards the Spanish troops, little dreaming, that day, of a general action. But the sound of a few shots caused me to return; and I found our line getting hastily under arms, and saw the enemy in motion. The prelude of skirmishing lasted about an hour and a half, and our division lost a few men by random gunshot; all this time we were standing at ease, and part of it exposed to a heavy, chilling, and comfortless rain. Sounds, however, which breathed all the fierceness of battle, soon reached us; the continued rolling of musketry, accompanied by loud and repeated discharges of cannon on our extreme right, told us, convincingly, that the real attack was in that quarter. The brigades of our division were successively called to support it. We formed in open column of companies at half-distance, and moved in rapid double quick to the scene of action. I remember well, as we: moved down in column, shot and shell flew over and through it in quick succession; we sustained little injury from either, but a captain of the Twenty-Ninth had been dreadfully lacerated by a ball, and lay directly in our path. We passed close to him, and he knew us all; and the heart-rending tone in which he called to us for water, or to kill him, I shall never forget. He lay alone, and we were in motion, and could give him no succour; for on this trying day, such of the wounded as could not walk, lay unattended where they fell:—all was hurry and struggle; every arm was wanted in the field. When we arrived near the discomfited and retiring Spaniards, and formed our line to advance through them towards the enemy, a very noble-looking young Spanish officer rode up to me, and begged me, with a sort of proud and brave anxiety, to explain to the English, that his countrymen were ordered to retire, but were not flying. Just as our line had entirely cleared the Spaniards, the smoky shroud of battle was, by the slackening of the fire, for one minute blown aside, and gave to our view the French grenadier caps, their arms, and the whole aspect of their frowning masses. It was a momentary, but a grand sight; a heavy atmosphere of smoke again enveloped us, and few objects could be discerned at all, none distinctly. The coolest and bravest soldier, if he be in the heat of it, can make no calculation of time during an engagement. Interested, and animated, he marks not the flight of the hours, but he feels that—

Come what come may,
Time and the hour run through the roughest day.

This murderous contest of musketry lasted long. We were the whole time progressively advancing upon and shaking the enemy. As the distance of about twenty yards from them, we received orders to charge; we had ceased firing, cheered, and had our bayonets in the charging position, when a body of the enemy's horse was discovered under the shoulder of a rising ground, ready to take advantage of our impetuosity. Already, however, had the French infantry, alarmed by our preparatory cheers, which always indicate the charge, broken and fled, abandoning some guns and howitzers about sixty yards from us. The presence of their cavalry not permitting us to pursue, we halted and recommenced firing on them. The slaughter was now, for a few minutes, dreadful; every shot told; their officers in vain attempted to rally them; they would make no effort. Some of their artillery, indeed, took up a distant position, which much annoyed our line; but we did not move, until we had expended every round of our ammunition, and then retired, in the most perfect order, to a spot sheltered from their guns, and lay down in line, ready to repulse any fresh attack with the bayonet. To describe my feelings throughout this wild scene with fidelity, would be impossible: at intervals, a shriek or groan told that men were falling around me; but it was not always that the tumult of the contest suffered me to catch these sounds. A constant feeling to the centre of the line, and the gradual diminution of our front, more truly bespoke the havoc of death.

As we moved, though slowly, yet ever a little in advance, our own killed and wounded lay behind us; but we arrived. among those of the enemy, and those of the Spaniards who had fallen in the first onset: we trod among the dead and dying, all reckless of them. But how shall I picture the British soldier going into action? He is neither heated by brandy, stimulated by the hope of plunder, or inflamed by the deadly feelings of revenge; he does not even indulge in expressions of animosity against his foes; he moves forward, confident of victory, never dreams of the possibility of defeat, and braves death with all the accompanying horrors of laceration. and torture, with the most cheerful intrepidity. Enough of joy and triumph. The roar of the battle is hushed; the hurry, of action is over; let us walk over the corpse-encumbered field. Look around,—behold thousands of slain, thousands of wounded, writhing with anguish, and groaning with agony and despair. Move a little this way, here lie four officers of the French Hundredth, all corpses.

Why, that boy cannot have numbered eighteen years! How beautiful, how serene a countenance! Perhaps, on the banks of the murmuring and peaceful Loire, some mother thinks anxiously of this her darling child. Here fought the third brigade; here the fusiliers: how thick these heroes lie! Most of the bodies are already stripped; rank is no longer distinguished. Yes: this must have been an officer; look at the delicate whiteness of his hands, and observe on his finger the mark of his ring. What manly beauty! what a smile still plays upon his lip! He fell, perhaps, beneath his colours; died easily; he is to be envied. Here charged the Polish lancers; not long ago, the trampling of horses, the shout, the cry, the prayer, the death-stroke, all mingled their wild sounds on this spot; it is now, but for a few fitful and stifled groans, as silent as the grave. What is this? A battered trumpet; the breath which filled, this morning, its haughty tone, has fled, perhaps, for ever. And here again, a broken lance. Is this the muscular arm that wielded it? 'Twas vigorous, and slew, perhaps, a victim on the field; it is now unnerved by death. Look at the contraction of this body, and the anguish of these features; eight times has some lance pierced this frame. Here again the headless trunks, and bodies torn and struck down by cannon shot; such death is sudden, horrid, but 'tis merciful. Who are these that catch every moment at our coats, and cling to our feet, in such a humble attitude? The wounded soldiers of the enemy, who are imploring British protection from the exasperated and revengeful Spaniards. What a proud compliment to our country!

Some readers will call this scene romantic, others disgusting: no matter; it is faithful; and it would be well for kings, politicians, and generals, if, while they talk of victories with exultation, and of defeats with philosophical indifference, they would allow their fancies to wander to the theatre of war, and the field of carnage. Incredible as it may appear, Marshal Beresford evidently thought a renewal of their attack, on the 17th, very possible; for he had us under arms two hours before break of day, and made arrangements, which certainly indicated any thing rather than intention to advance. It is to be presumed, that could the marshal have guessed the dreadful slaughter he had made in the ranks of the enemy, and their consequent disorganization and discontent, he would have entered the wood, to which they retired on the evening of the sixteenth, and thus have achieved a more complete triumph than any up to that period gained in the Peninsula. Report said that Blake very strongly urged this measure. Our army was indubitably equal to an affair on the evening of the sixteenth: we had been reinforced by a British brigade under the orders of Colonel Kemmis, who arrived after the battle; the casualties of our German light battalions had been trifling; our Portuguese division was quite fresh, as were two Spanish divisions; and our cavalry, an arm most ably commanded by General Lumley, had sustained little or no loss; and all the troops were much animated by what they had witnessed.

Had Wellington commanded on this day, he would have altogether destroyed the army of Soult, and captured the whole of his *matériel* and the men, who fought in the ranks of the two distinguished brigades I had occasion to particularise, in my general sketch of the action, would not now, perhaps, have had the mortification of walking, unnoticed and undecorated, by the side of the more fortunate heroes of Waterloo. The whole of the seventeenth we never ventured across the stream, but stood looking at the enemy's picquets, and videttes, posted impudently on the little plain between us and their bivouack. On the eighteenth they retired, destroying the contents of many of their tumbrils and ammunition cars, to facilitate the conveyance of their wounded; and they were followed, at a respectful distance, by our cavalry and light infantry. It was not until the nineteenth, that is, three days, after the battle, that we occupied the wood to which the enemy, after their bloody defeat, had been driven in discomfiture and confusion.

Our wounded were removed, with as much expedition as possible, to Valverde; but the field hospitals, for two or three days after the engagement, presented scenes, at the recollection of which humanity quite shudders. I never can forget seeing, on the twentieth, the small chapel at Albuera filled with French wounded, very great numbers of whom had suffered amputation, and who lay on the hard stones, without even straw, in a dirty, comfortless state; all which was unavoidably the case, for we had nothing to give them on the spot, and, owing to the want of conveyances, they were forced to wait till our own people had been carried to the rear.

This same day I again went down to that part of the field, which was covered with the slain; they, lay ghastly and unburied: here and there, indeed, you might remark a loose-made grave, where some officers or soldiers had been to perform an act of private friendship. I was much struck with one affecting, though simple proof of the attachment of our peninsular allies: the hands of vast numbers of the British corpses had been clasped together in the attitude of prayer, and placed by the Spaniards in the manner they superstitiously imagine it important to lay out their dead.

On the 22nd we marched upon Solano, and the 23rd resumed our old quarters at Almendralejo. We found here three hundred French soldiers, all wounded, who had been left in a convent, and recommended to our protection. Several hundred prisoners were made, at the different cantonments of the army, under similar circumstances; but General Gazan carried four thousand wounded to Seville in safety. The Hon. William Stewart, our division general, paid great attention to such of the enemy as were left in Almendralejo; he almost daily visited their hospitals, and satisfied himself, by personal inquiries, whether they were properly taken care of. I have more than once been present at these visits, and the gratitude of these poor fellows was strongly pictured on their countenances, and in every thing they said. In speaking of their own commanders, they called Soult blood-thirsty and avaricious, saying that he cared not how he sacrificed his men, and that he was wholly bent on the pursuit of dignities and wealth.

On the 25th of May, General Lumley had a brilliant affair

with the enemy's cavalry, near Usagre; and conducting it, as he did every thing, both with skill and intrepidity, he overthrew and routed them, though very superior in number, sabring several on the spot, and taking nearly one hundred prisoners. The detachment captured was composed entirely of French Heavy Dragoons, of the 4th, 20th, and 26th Regiments: many of them were severely cut over the head and face; but they were, with few exceptions, fine soldier-like looking men, who had apparently seen a great deal of service; and. they all wore that warlike helmet, which I,have before mentioned, and which we have since adopted.

CHAPTER 11

French Prisoners

During the whole time that we remained stationary at Al-mendralejo, the siege of Badajos was carried on, under the direction of Wellington in person, by two divisions of the army of the north, which had come from Beira to strengthen us in this quarter. Two gallant assaults were made on the fort of San Christoval, the possession of which would have secured the reduction of the place. Our troops displayed great courage, but were repulsed.[15] On the 10th of June the siege was raised; for it was known that Marshal Marmont was breaking up from the environs of Ciudad Rodrigo, and about to form a junction with Soult, for the relief of Badajos. On the 11th we retired from Al-mendralejo, on the 14th and 15th we bivouacked near Albuera, and on the 17th we forded the Guadiana, about three leagues to the south of Badajos, and marched upon Elvas. On the line of march this day, I saw a body of the Estremaduran legion; a corps raised, clothed, and commanded by a General Downie, an Englishman, who had formerly been a commissary in our service. Anything so whimsical or ridiculous as the dress of this corps, I never beheld: it was meant to be an imitation of the ancient costume of Spain. The turned-up hat, slashed doublet, and short mantle, might have figured very well in the play of Pizarro, or at an exhibition of Astley's; but in the rude and ready bivouack, they appeared absurd and ill-chosen. In the midst of our misery and discomfort, the same evening, we could not avoid laughing

15. Their repulse was caused by obstacles which no valour could overcome.

at the recollection of these poor devils, who, in their fantastic dresses, must have been exposed to the same violent storm which extinguished our fires, soaked our ground, and, forcing its way through our tents, drenched us to the skin.

On the 18th we were moved into Elvas, to get a drying and a night's rest under cover. Many of our wounded officers and men were in hospital, or billets in this town, and the day was of course quite a holiday of the heart to us all. It was a strange thing to see, in the crowded wards of the hospitals, English and French soldiers lying helplessly side by side, or here and there performing little kind offices for each other, with a willing and a cheerful air. Their wants and thoughts, I observed, they communicated to each other in phrases of Spanish, which language many of the French privates spoke fluently, and our men understood well enough for all common purposes.

On the 19th we marched to the banks of the Caya, and were placed in position at a spot called Torre-de-Moro, about two leagues from Elvas, and directly on the frontier. We remained here until the 21st of July, leading a regular, healthful, pleasing camp life. For one week, indeed, our regiment being on an advanced post, and distributed in three very pretty gardens; the foot of a large thick-spreading mulberry-tree, a fountain of clear water sparkling near it, was my happy and tranquil resting-place. Disposed of in Campo Mayor, or bivouacked in situations to admit of their being readily brought together, lay almost all the divisions of the allied army; and am the banks of the Caya, I imagine, we should certainly have fought, had the enemy attempted to pass that river. Their superiority of numbers, however, especially in cavalry, had rendered it impossible for us to hazard any thing on the plains of Spanish Estremadura.

On the 22nd of June, Soult and Marmont made a strong reconnaissance; but their object in saving Badajos having been gained, they made no further demonstration. About the middle of July, Marmont returned with his people to the north; and Lord Wellington, crossing the Tagus at Villa Velha, marched to Beira, leaving the troops under General Hill cantoned in

Alentejo. From the 22nd of July to the third of September, our division lay at Villa Viçosa, a handsome well-built town, about five leagues from Elvas. A hunting-palace; a fine large preserve, walled in, and filled with deer, and game; wide streets, handsome houses, a royal chapel, and several churches and convents, attest the former rank of this town, which was once a favourite country retreat for the court of Portugal. Our billets here were very comfortable; the walks and rides in the park, which, from the inequalities of the ground, and the thickness of the underwood, had all the character of a wilderness, were strikingly beautiful; the markets well supplied, and the vineyards of Borba, so celebrated for its wine, lay within two miles of us.

One of my daily amusements was attendance at the royal chapel, where the music and singing were both very excellent. Often, indeed, would the organist introduce into his voluntaries the most touching airs, and, sometimes, airs of too tender and voluptuous a character for the solemnity of a church. During my stay in this town, I was one day attracted by the sight; of, an unusual crowd at the chapel of a convent, and on entering it I found, that a. lady, having completed her year as noviciate, was then taking the veil. I arrived so late, and was so distant from the altar, that I saw nothing of the ceremony; but I heard the faint sound of a soft pleasing voice; the utterance was tremulous and indistinct; the words were quite lost. A bystander told me that the unfortunate female had then pronounced her vow. The most breathless silence had prevailed while the noviciate had, spoken; the deep voice of a priest replied, and seemed to confirm her vow by a short prayer. To this succeeded an anthem, sweetly sung by the sisters, and in parts of which, all the priests and many of the congregation devoutly joined. The notes of praise and thanksgiving sounded proud and joyous. The altars, shrines, and. walls of the chapel were all decorated with flowers; and, as the crowd came out, you might observe all the relations of the youthful victim dressed gaily, as on a festival. I felt quite oppressed with melancholy; and the brilliant scene, and animated music, so ill according with a sacrifice at the altar, like that I had just witnessed, struck me to the very soul. In the grave we only deposit the lifeless and insensible body, but when we devote youth, affection, and reason to the cheerless cloister, we bury and entomb the heart. Such is the cruel perversion of monastic institutions; in which, if they served only as the retreats of deserted age, disappointment, and sorrow, we should find little, perhaps nothing, to condemn.

From Villa Viçosa we moved to Portalegre, a favourite and often-visited quarter. About this time, some movements of a French division under the orders of General Girard, who had crossed the Guadiana at Merida, and was insulting and foraging the northern district of Estremadura, rendering it necessary for us to take the field, the division was assembled in bivouack, near the village of Codiceira, oh the 22nd of October. The weather, I well remember, was on that night so severe, that three Portuguese soldiers died on the ground from the effect of the heavy and pouring rain. After some marches and manoeuvres, which were well and quietly conducted, we arrived at dusk, on the evening of the 27th, at the village of Alcuescar, distant only four miles from the small town of Arroyo de Molinos, where the division of Girard slept that night, in fearless but mistaken security. We lay upon our arms, without fires, about six hours; and at two in the morning of the 28th, we moved forward, in profound silence, by a narrow bad road, upon Arroyo de Molinos, near which town we halted, at half-past six, on ground highly favourable both to our formation and concealment.

We were here divided into three columns. The first brigade was directed straight forwards on the town; our own, with one of Portuguese, made a rapid circuitous march to the right of it, and arrived, under cover of fog and rain, within a few yards of the road, by which alone the enemy could retire, and on which he was then forming, preparatory to his march, in profound ignorance of our approach: our cavalry moved in the centre ready to act as occasion might require.

The cheers of the first brigade, which entered the town charging, and bayoneted, drove, or captured his rear-guard, first announced to the enemy his imminent and unexpected danger. He would have rapidly retired: in vain; our cavalry galloped forwards, dispersed, sabred, and made prisoners his few horse, who, after attempting some formation on the left of the infantry, which stood for a moment in a posture of defence, fled in great confusion. About two hundred yards behind the spot, where the enemy's columns were formed on the plain, rose the rocky and precipitous Sierra de Montanches, and to this, on seeing our brigade advancing rapidly upon them, they ran with unresisting panic. We followed them closely, and scrambling among the rocks, quite mixed with them, and made prisoners at every step; until the number of pursuers being diminished by exhaustion and fatigue; and being encumbered with arms, ammunition, and knapsacks, all which, such of the enemy as escaped, threw from them, we desisted from the pursuit.

A general of cavalry, the Prince D'Aremberg, (a colonel of chasseurs, and a connection of Napoleon's,) a chief of the staff, two lieutenant-colonels, thirty officers, and about twelve hundred privates, taken prisoners, together with the capture of a half brigade of artillery, and all their baggage, rewarded bur fatigues and privations, and we returned in high spirits to Arroyo. The French sustained some loss from the fire of the first brigade, and some from the guns, which accompanied that column; but our share of the business, among the rocks, was a scene of laughter and diversion, rather than of bloodshed and peril; for though some of the enemy's grenadiers discharged their muskets at us before they broke them, still our loss was very trifling, and the danger too inconsiderable to be thought or spoken of.

We had here a most amusing specimen of French character: in the French column one of the regiments was numbered Thirty-Four; in the British column also the Thirty-Fourth Regiment led the pursuit, and got quite mixed with the enemy. Several of the French officers, as they tendered their swords, embraced the officers of the English thirty-fourth, saying,—

"*Ah, Messieurs, nous sommes des frères, nous sommes du trente-quatrième régiment tous deux.*"—

"*Vous êtes des braves.*"—

"*Les Anglois se battent toujours avec loyauté, et traitent bien leurs prisonniers.*"—

"*Ah, Messieurs, la fortune de la guerre est bien capricieuse.*"—

Under any circumstances, however unfortunate, this people will find some method of disarming wrath, courting favour, and softening their fate:—they have spirits, too, wonderfully elastic; and have the readiest ingenuity in framing excuses for any disaster, or disgrace, which may befall them. I was on duty over the prisoners, a few days after the affair; at the close of the day's march a chapel was allotted to them for the night, and to have seen them take possession of it, one really would have thought that they were still marching free, and in arms; they entered it, singing, "*Grenadiers, ici; grenadiers, ici*"—"*Voltigeurs, là, là; voltigeurs, là, là*"—and ran tumultuously, the grenadiers to the altar, and the voltigeurs to the gallery. In ten minutes all were at home—some playing cards, some singing, some dancing—here a man was performing Punch, behind a great coat, with infinite drollery—there again, quieter men were occupied in repairing their clothes or shoes, while in one part of the chapel a self-elected orator was addressing a group on their late capture, in such terms, as, "*Messieurs, vous n'êtes pas déshonorés*"—

"*On nous a trompé; cet espion, cet Espagnol, nous a vendu.*"—

"*Et comment! qui vous a dit cela?*" said a rough voice.—

"*Monsieur,*" replied my orator, "*vous me permettrez de savoir. Je suis de Paris même, et je connois la guerre.*"—

This speech was highly approved; for several vociferated—"*Ah! oui, il a raison; nous avons été vendus par ce vilain espion.*"

"*Nous aurions battu les Anglois dans une affaire rangée, mais certainment,*" said my little Parisian; and just then, the rations, making their appearance, they all hurried to the door, and singing some song, the chorus of which was "*Bonne soupe, bonne soupe,*" they eagerly took their meat, and set about preparing it.

I should lose sight, however, of the French military character, if I omitted to notice, that several of the serjeants and old soldiers who were decorated and wore the chevrons of service, appeared exceedingly sulky, and vented their anger in a sort of muttering smothered swearing. Those who have seen a ferocious Frenchman utter from, between his closed teeth his favourite oath of "*Sacré Dieu!*" will agree that there are few things more savage and offensive. The troops taken at Arroyo were all remarkably, fine men, selected for the service on which they had been employed. Girard escaped himself with the small remains of a brigade; and, most fortunately for him, the first brigade of his division had marched at five in the morning under General Remond, or it would probably have shared the same fate as that under his immediate command, Soult placed Girard in arrest when he rejoined the army of the south, and made a, most severe report of his neglect and misconduct to the emperor; but Girard was a favourite with Buonaparte, and got through this affair without the loss of head or commission. Napoleon understood the character of his officers, and knew when and whom to pardon, foreseeing whose gratitude and services would be valuable.

At the battle of Lutzen, in the year 1813, General Girard displayed great ability, and gave a bright example of his zeal, devotion, and courage; for, although severely wounded and covered with blood, he refused to be taken from the fields declaring aloud, that the moment was then arrived, when every true Frenchman should conquer or die on the ground on which he fought. One thing in our success at Arroyo de Molinos gratified our division highly; it was a triumph for our general, a triumph all his own. He gained great credit for this well-conducted enterprise, and he gained what, to one of his mild, kind, and humane character, was still more valuable, a solid and a bloodless victory; for it is certainly the truest, maxim in war, "that conquest is twice achieved, where the achiever brings home full numbers."

After these operations, our division returned to Portalegre, and, towards the close of November, an order from England to proceed to India, called me, for a time from a corps, a service, and a country, to all of which I felt a very strong attachment. With spirits much depressed, myself and a brother officer, destined also to join the first battalion, set out on our sorrowful journey to Lisbon, on the morning of the 27th of November. If I except the adventures of one evening, our route to Lisbon presented no occurrence of sufficient interest to impress my memory.

In attempting to ride a nearer road from Garfete to Abrantes, than that which led by Gaviao, we lost our way, and were obliged to put up for the night in a poor goat-herd's hut. We here, however, witnessed a scene of domestic happiness and patriarchal manners, which gave us reason to rejoice that we had slept under such a roof. The family consisted of a venerable old peasant, his, daughter, a woman of about four-and-thirty, and her five children: the eldest, a most beautiful girl of fifteen; and the youngest, a fine black-eyed boy of eight. The husband of this woman was absent on a journey; the old peasant was not within; and when we first entered, the mother and her children were at supper: they pressed us to partake of it; we declined, but procured from them some fine rich goat's milk; and boiling it up with bread of Indian corn, made an excellent meal. It was late when the old man came in from his labour; he expressed great delight at our having rested in his cot, as, he said, there was no house within two leagues of that spot, the night dark and stormy, and the road bad and dangerous. A small wooden bowl of vegetable soup was brought him for his supper; he crossed himself and said a short grace; but my astonishment was not a little excited, by observing, that during the whole time he was eating his frugal meal, the family all stood up; and with their hands closed and lifted up, and their eyes raised towards the crucifix, prayed; not with extravagant fervour, nor as if it were a tame unmeaning form, but with much natural feeling, and seemed to invoke blessings on the head of this, the respected elder of their cottage.

The old man, too, however habitual it might be, appeared deeply impressed with the ceremony, and took his food with a sort of quiet, solemn thankfulness. The expression of the grand-daughter's countenance, who seemed much attached to him, was really seraphic; and I thought the whole scene quite a subject for a painting. In general, the beauty of people, in a common class of life, carries with it a stamp of vulgarity, for which it is difficult to account, but which checks admiration. Here it was far otherwise. An expressive eye of the deepest blue, an elegant contour of countenance, dark clustering ringlets, and a perfect form, would have made this cottage girl remarkable anywhere; and she would have been gazed on with interest as well as pleasure, amid the most brilliant assemblies of a capital or a court. When we lay down for the night, all the children knelt at the feet of their grandfather and received his blessing, sealed by him with a kiss upon their young foreheads. I slept with a sort of sweet and superstitious confidence under this happy roof; so much, and so pleasingly, had I been effected by the simplicity of manners, among its poor contented inmates.

In the morning, after literally forcing on them a small present, we set forward highly gratified, and took a very pleasant bridle-path to Abrantes, where we embarked for Lisbon. Here we were detained a considerable time waiting for a passage, a circumstance most vexatious and provoking; for with the prospect before us of a long banishment and a remote service, we were naturally eager to avail ourselves of every spare moment we might enjoy in England, prior to the sailing of the fleet for India.

Our detention at Lisbon, though during the greater part of December, gave us an opportunity of being present at the gay and splendid festival of Christmas eve. At the dark and gloomy hour of midnight, on the 24th of December, the whole population of that crowded city is alert and in motion, Tapers blaze in every hand, and, dressed in their gayest attire, all persons hasten to the churches, which are open, fancifully decorated with superb hangings, and brilliantly illuminated. Here, the natal day of our Saviour is ushered in with all the peculiarities and pomp of Catholic worship. The music, the incense, the innumerable lights, the delighted devotion of the kneeling multitudes, and the loud and swelling hymns, which close the ceremony of this midnight mass, produce an effect, which acts too powerfully on the senses. The more I see of the Roman Catholic religion, the less am I surprised that the people of southern Europe, who are certainly both impassioned and imaginative, should attach themselves to a

134

church, the forms and ceremonies of which, addressing both the senses and the fancy, make, to them, the attendance on public worship a business of pleasure, as well as of duty. The scenic representations of Gospel history, which, on high fasts and festivals, are to be met with in almost all the churches of the Peninsula, however ridiculous they may appear, are not without their use; for to them (most inadequate, I admit, to their purpose) the poorer classes are, nevertheless, indebted for much of the instruction they receive, concerning the life and miracles of the divine Founder of our blessed faith.

It was on the 29th day of December, 1811, that I sailed from the Tagus for England, and it was early in the month of August, 1812, that, having escaped my banishment to India, by a fortunate and well-timed promotion. I landed once more on the Quay of Lisbon. The glorious news of the victory of Salamanca greeted me on my arrival. The joy of the Portuguese at this signal triumph, so honourable to their troops, as well as our own, knew no bounds. Masses, processions, illuminations, and new overtures and marches in honour of it, performed night after night, in crowded theatres, bespoke their patriotic pleasure. The consummate skill displayed by Wellington in this memorable engagement, was, to a soldier again about to enter camps under his command, a proud and flattering augury of success; and, in spite of all the croaking I had been compelled to listen to in England, made me look forward with a confident hope, to an honourable and glorious conclusion of this interesting war. Nor, as an ardent admirer of the Spanish character, was my opinion of their courage and constancy at all shaken. It is true their armies and their garrisons had met with great, but not surprising misfortunes; I say not surprising, because the military man of professional experience could not have expected that the half-organized and ill-commanded armies of Spain would successfully oppose the victorious and veteran legions of a renowned military power in the open field, or in the more difficult operations of regular warfare. Their armies were beaten in almost every engagement, and their fortresses, though often bravely defended, fell one after the other into the hands of the invaders. Want of skill in some of their leaders, and treachery in others, to whose reputed talents they had blindly and helplessly yielded up the task of directing their courage, led to these fatal misfortunes; but Spain, that is, the country, the people, still resisted. The inhabitants of towns and cities occupied by the French, secretly contributed money for this purpose, and were ever ready to convey useful information to their brethren in arms.

The brave peasants inhabiting all their mountainous districts, disbanded soldiers, and spirited volunteers, from every part of Spain, rallied around chieftains, whose hearty and valiant efforts in the cause were daily crowned with partial, but highly useful successes. In Catalonia, Navarre, Arragon, and Biscay, Eroles, Lacy, and Mina commanded large bodies of guerillas, equally formidable from their surprising activity, and their undaunted courage. In the very heart of Spain, Empecinado, at the head of a bold and loyal peasantry, spread terror to the very gates of Madrid; while Don Julian Sanchez led his enter-prizing horse into Old Castile, and, though surrounded by their principal establishments, daily captured their convoys and supplies, and kept their cantonments in a constant state of anxiety and alarm. No:—the efforts of the Spaniards to deliver themselves from the yoke of France must never be forgotten; and no man of generosity or of candour would willingly cast a shade over their heroic exertions. They had no government, no ministers, no generals; yet, under all these disadvantages, they ever remained true to the cause; and it is to their partial and continual struggles against the French detachments scattered over the face of their country, that we are indebted for our ultimate success. Had not the forces of the enemy been so constantly employed, and their communications so often menaced by the active hatred of the Spanish people, it is vain to suppose, that even the ability and genius of a Wellington, or the discipline and intrepidity of a British army, (which, however excellent in composition, was numerically feeble,) could have long resisted the combinations of eight marshals of France, and the efforts of two hundred thousand soldiers.

While my mind thus fondly dwells upon the patriotism of the Spanish people, how does my heart sink within me to think of their present wrongs, their wretchedness, their degradation! and all this heaped upon their heads by the very monarch they bled to liberate and restore. But I am consoled by the firm belief, that the Spaniards will soon awaken the eyes of their monarch to the injustice, the cruelty, and the misrule of his detested advisers; or will, by one mighty effort, free themselves from his odious tyranny, and place the sceptre of their beauteous land in abler and more virtuous hands.

The news of this battle of Salamanca made me anxious to join my regiment, still under General Hill, with as much expedition as possible, for it was natural to suppose that this event, and Lord Wellington's advance into the very heart of Spain, would either compel Soult to raise the siege of Cadiz, and retire from Andalusia, or would lead to some offensive movements on our part to free the south from the presence of the enemy.

CHAPTER 12

Return to the Regiment

I left Lisbon for Estremadura, happily unencumbered by any detachment. At Abrantes I met a column of three thousand of the prisoners taken at Salamanca. They were in a very exhausted state, from the length of their march, the heat of the weather, and the want of shoes and other necessaries; and, unlike my friends at Arroyo-de-Molinos, they had neither a word or a laugh to disguise their mortification. I never saw Frenchmen more thoroughly cut down; and, what appeared not a little to increase their vexation, they were escorted by four hundred awkward-looking, ill-appointed Portuguese militia-men, whose air of pride and importance, as they regulated the motions of these *"vainqueurs d'Austerlitz,"* was truly entertaining. It is not generous to exult over fallen foes, but it is difficult to pity them, when your eyes have rested on scenes of desolation and ruin caused by many, perhaps, whose appearance would otherwise interest you in their favour. Not a town or a village had I passed, on my route from Lisbon, but affecting traces of the invasion of this smiling country were every where to be seen. Cottages all roof-less and untenanted, the unpruned vine, growing in rank luxuriance over their ruined walls, neglected gardens, the shells of fine houses, half destroyed by fire, convents and churches, too solid to be demolished, standing open and neglected, with the ornamental wood or stone work, which once adorned them, broken down and defaced; all proclaimed silently, but forcibly, that I was travelling through a country which had been the theatre of war, and exposed to the ravages of contending armies. Such are the scenes which, not only in Portugal, but throughout Spain, arrest the eye at every step, and make the Briton, while he sighs over the miseries of the peaceful citizens, and laborious peasants, whose towns and villages have been thus visited by violence and rapine, offer up many a grateful prayer for the secure and heaven-defended position of his happier countrymen.

From Abrantes I travelled alone, and in great comfort; every morning, after journeying about two leagues, in some pleasant spot, under a shady tree near a stream, or by some solitary chapel or fountain, I halted for an hour, had my baggage unloaded, my animals unsaddled and fed, and making a fire to boil my kettle, sat down in great comfort to my breakfast. I carried up the country with me this time a collection of about fifty volumes, which my friend and messmate had directed me to purchase for him in London. The best of the British poets and classics were of the number, and oftentimes would I lounge over a favourite author till the heat of the day was gone by, and pursue my route to the town, where I proposed sleeping, in the cool of the evening.

A large wood, on my road from Altera de Chaõ to Monforte, was said to be much infested by robbers, and I was advised not to ride that stage alone; however, I felt protected by my uniform, and set forward, halting midway to breakfast, as usual. I took a post in a most romantic and sequestered spot, about a quarter of a mile from the roadside, near a natural fountain, from which the water welled forth with a soft and soothing sound. It was not until I was already seated at my breakfast, that I discovered at the foot of a dark mass of rock-stone, very near me, one of those rude wooden crosses, always erected in this country, to denote the spot where accidental, sudden, or violent death has overtaken some wretched traveller. It had scratched on it a very recent date, and in spite of the attractions of Johnson's Rasselas, and a good breakfast, I will own that I swallowed my meal with what haste and appetite I could, and again set forward. However, my day's ride passed over very quietly; I had not the bad fortune, or good, as some would have considered it, to meet with any *banditti,* or even an adventure, if I except encountering, in a dark and narrow glen, a monk and a muleteer, who came pricking on at a sober pace, and gave me full time to decide, that they might have sat very well for Schedoni and Spalatro, and would have made an admirable frontispiece to *Miss Radcliffe's Italian.*

It was not without a feeling of deep and mournful interest, that, on the evening I halted at Badajos, I walked round the walls of that deadly-purchased fortress. At the time I saw it, the works were rapidly repairing; but the town presented a wretched appearance, most of the loftier buildings, and all those near the breaches, having been demolished by the fire of our batteries. The murderous assault of the 6th of April must have been dreadful to look upon. At the main breach alone, upwards of two thousand men are said to have fallen, and, at this point, not one soul penetrated into the town. Some of our officers, who were wounded, and taken on the breach, and carried through it, represented it as provided with defences, through which the most intrepid soldiers could never have forced their way; a ditch, cutting it off from the body of the place, a breast-work, and strong *chevaux-de-frize* of sword-blades were the obstacles opposed to us, and to these must be added a heavy and incessant fire of musketry. The escalade at the castle was a fine bold effort, and was indeed eminently successful. Some outworks also were carried at the bayonet's point in a gallant style; and the division, which penetrated into the town by the bastion of San Vincente, deserves uncommon credit.

I leant long and silently over the parapet at that angle by which it ascended. What a scene, on the night of the 6th of April, must these walls have presented! Blazing cressets, fire balls, rockets, the explosion of shells, and the red flashes of cannon and musketry, must have spread around a terrific illumination; terrific, for it lighted up a scene of wild confusion and reeking slaughter. The reports of cannon, the rattle of musketry, the shouts of the assailants, and the drums and trumpets of the garrison, were the sounds which, that night, scared sleep from the pillows of the wretched citizens; and the huzza of victory was to them the prelude of a scene of violence and plunder. Happy are ye, my countrymen, who read only of these things, and are spared such trials! How cheerful, how grateful should ye be to that presiding Power, which keeps from your humble and boasted castles, war and its dark train of miseries! In the morning, before I left the city, as I was passing a large church, I heard the sound of hammers and anvils, and, on entering, I found that this handsome building had been converted by the French, during the siege, into a work-shop; by us it had still been applied to the same purpose, and there, where a peaceful congregation had often met to offer up their prayers, blacksmiths, armourers, and carpenters, were now busily occupied in their noisy labours.

On my road to Zafra I stopped, for one hour, in the ruined village of Albuera, and walked alone over the field. Some redoubts had been lately constructed on it by General Hill, as a measure of precaution, in the event of his corps ever being compelled to fight upon this ground; but for these works, there was nothing which spoke of war, or soldiers. All was rural and sunny, and silent. No marks of feet, or hoofs, upon the plain! the grass grew thick and strong, and wild flowers were springing from that turf, which had been moistened by valour's purest blood. Not a vestige of the memorable battle remained. As I was mounting to pursue my journey, a rude inscription, scratched with charcoal on the chapel wall, caught my eye; it ran thus:

La Guerre en Espagne est la Fortune des Géneraux, l'Ennui des Officiers, et le Tombeau des Soldats.

It was in this same chapel, fifteen months before, that I had seen several hundred French prisoners, many of whom were dying, and all of whom were dreadfully wounded, stretched in their last agonies, and groaning with anguish. How painfully and faithfully illustrative of the truth of this brief inscription, was the scene with which my memory then supplied me. I passed the night at the pretty village of Almendral; near this place, as I learned from my host, a wealthy intelligent peasant, a French corps, under the orders of Marshal Mortier, had been for some weeks bivouacked in the year 1811. In speaking of the strict discipline maintained by Mortier, and of the protection he gave them, and their property, my host used a very strong expression; for he styled him the father of the peasants. This quite corresponded with the language of the French soldiers about this same Marshal, and hearty was the blessing which I bestowed on this respected name. Yes, although we shrink from the mention of some French leaders, who appear to have gloried in oppression and cruelty, it cannot be denied that many high-minded and honourable men have marched with the armies of France; and while some of my countrymen inveigh against all the French military with undistinguishing severity, they would do well to recollect, that a soldier cannot, under any government, choose his service, or be held responsible for the justice of that war in which he may chance to be employed. How many Englishmen served on the expedition against Copenhagen, with distinction and honour, who may have considered it a daring act of aggression, justifiable on the doctrine of expediency alone? an argument we seldom admit when speaking of the actions or politics of an enemy.

At the village of Santa Martha, I again entered the high road. This wretched place was in a sad condition; for it had been occupied, alternately, by French and English, several times in the course of the spring and summer, and its resources were completely exhausted. Provisions were dear and scarce; and, on every side, poverty and want assailed you with imploring prayers. It was really heart-breaking to look upon the squalid appearance of the children, which is always more affecting than that of grown beggars; for childhood is the season of careless and playful joy, and to see the roses on their young cheeks blighted by the icy touch of famine, is peculiarly distressing.

On the road from Santa Martha to Zafra, you pass a town called Feria, which is beautifully situated on the side of a lofty hill on your right, from the summit of which a Moorish fort and tower, still frowning, though decayed, look nobly down, and speak to the reflecting traveller, of men, and days, and deeds, now, as a tale, gone by.

In Zafra, I once more embraced my brother officers, and found myself at home. Wander where he will, a regiment is ever, to a single man, the best of homes. There is no manner of life, which so effectually conceals from us the cheerlessness and the helplessness of celibacy, as the desultory life of a soldier. For him, who, by the want of fortune or other controlling circumstances, is debarred the exquisite happiness of reposing his aching heart on that blessed resting-place, the bosom of a wife, —for such a man there is no life, save one of travel or of military occupation, which can excite feelings of interest or consolation. The hazard of losing life, which a soldier is often called on to encounter, give to his existence, as often as it is preserved, a value, it would, otherwise, soon cease to possess. Frequent change of country and of scene, enliven and divert your thoughts; and if it is painful at a certain age, to think, that, when you fall, no widow, no child, will drop a tear over your grave,—it is, on the other hand, a comfort to know, that none are dependant on your existence; that none will be left unprovided and in misery at your death.

Zafra is a fine town, built at the foot of a high and steep hill, from the summit of which you command a very extensive view of mountain scenery. Near Zafra are the remains of a large and handsome convent, once the pride and the boast of the city. The French have entirely destroyed it: on one of its ruined walls, I saw "*Compagnie d'élite du vingtseptième dragons,*" marked in chalk. This monastery, however, was one of those which had been erected within the last century, was not hallowed by antiquity, and the sight, therefore, of its tottering ruins excited no feeling, but one of pleasure, unmingled with regret, and undisturbed by any recollection of interest.

The evening after my arrival in this quarter I went to a ball given by some British officer of rank. The country-dances now in use among the Spaniards, and introduced, I imagine, either by the French or Germans, are all in waltz time and to waltz movements; they are uncommonly graceful. There were some very pretty women at this assembly. My worthy countrymen do not shine in the soft and pleasing movements of the waltz; they deserve, however, to be laughed at, for why do they not sit still? I really quite pitied some of the Spanish girls, whose eyes, heads, arms, and indeed, whole frames, seemed to move in voluptuous unison with the music, when I saw their waists encircled by the arms of awkward, ungraceful partners. In the course of the evening, a handsome young Spaniard and a pretty-made little girl, danced for us the *bolero*. This beautiful dance is too well known to need description; it has much of the ballet character; is very expressive, and tells quite a. little, tale of love. The sound of the castanets, too, with which the motion of it are always accompanied, is both cheerful and animating.

I found by the news here, that Lord Wellington had entered Madrid on the 12th, in triumph; and that Joseph Buonaparte had retired upon Valencia. Soult was making preparations to evacuate Andalusia; and it was conjectured, that he would march through Grenada and Murcia, and probably join the King.

On the 28th of August, we marched on the Seville road, to Bienvenida, On the following day, we proceeded to Ilerena; we here received accounts, that Colonel Skerret had entered Seville, and that the French had taken the route of Cordova. Our movement southward was stopped at the small town of Ayllones; and we counter-marched on the Guadiana, passing by Maguilla, el Campillo, and Zalamea, to Quintana, where we halted three, and then to a village about ten miles from the Guadiana, where we remained seven days. This short halt was probably to await the instructions of Wellington.

On the 13th, the corps was again in motion; and my brigade marched to the city of Medellin. On the high ground, before you descend to the river, on which this city is built, you enjoy one of those grand and sublime views, which fix themselves for ever in the imagination; and of which the recollection is so lasting and so delightful. To the right is seen the bold Sierra de Guadalupe, and behind it, many a lofty range of mountains, which rise one above the other in rude majesty, ever varying to the eye of the moving traveller, in form, and height, and hue. To the left, less distant and not so lofty, rise the abrupt and precipitous Sierras de Montanches; below you, the rich vale of the Guadiana, populous and fertile, lies smiling with corn fields and vineyards, among which, several white towns and villages are scattered in the most pleasing sites. The town of Medellin is very ancient, and not well built. A large citadel, which it once boasted, is now a heap of useless ruins; it is famous, however, for having given birth to the celebrated Hernan Cortez, the bold and adventurous conqueror of Mexico. They pretend to shew the very house in which he was born, and in which, three hundred years ago, he played about a disregarded child; as a young man, being idle, dissipated, and unruly, he so irritated his father, that the old man drove him in anger from his peaceful roof. Such was the origin, and such the early life of this wonderful man, upon whose exploits posterity has dwelt with so much admiration, and for whose atrocities it has so often indignantly blushed.

In the evening, I walked over that field, which, in the spring of 1809, proved so fatal to the Spaniards. This battle was most rashly and presumptuously courted on disadvantageous ground; and as naturally as deservedly lost. The victims in this disastrous battle were never buried; no charity able hands were near to perform this last kind office; at every step, human bones, bleached by the sun and wind, lay scattered in my path. It was painful and humiliating to carry the mind back to the slow decay of the manly bodies which once covered them—bodies, in which the full tide of youth, and health, and spirits, was stopped suddenly and for ever, and which had lain all exposed to the wolf of the mountains, and the eagle of the rock, who left the cavern and the cliff, to make their feast on man!

On the 14th we marched to Escurial, on the 15th to Santa Cruz. The situation of this last village is very beautiful, and the neighbourhood highly picturesque. Above it rises a proud majestic mountain, whose broad sides, towards the base, are clothed with the olive and the vine in rich profusion, while the higher region has a crown of heath, and rock-stone, most beautifully variegated with colourings, such as the art of the painter would in vain attempt to imitate.

On the 16th we marched to Truxillo, once a considerable city, filled with palaces and convents, and reckoning above eight hundred inhabited houses. It had been one of the richest and most flourishing commercial cities in the interior of Spain. The decay of trade gave the first blow to its prosperity, and the French, in a three months' residence, completed its destruction. Of seventeen palaces only two remain inhabited, and five hundred houses empty, deserted, and fast falling to decay, only remind you of what it once was, what it no longer is. It still, however. looks nobly in the distance, and, ere you reach the walls, you imagine you are about to enter a magnificent city. On a hill above it stand the solid remains of a Roman castle, said by the priests to have been built by Julius Caesar. Now, to be sure, the priests in Spain know very little about these matters; but it matters not whether I was deceived; I, for the time, enjoyed the pleasure of fancying, as I walked over the ruin, that the foot of Caesar had once rested where I trod. The tottering walls of some later works adjoining it, shew that it has, since those days, been a station of the Moors. In the square of Truxillo stands a large, noble-looking mansion, once the residence of the family of Pizarro, and built, probably, out of the rich and precious spoils of injured and insulted Peru. The sculpture and relief which adorn the front of this building, tell, with fidelity, the tale of the founder, but in a manner very revolting to the feelings of an Englishman. Peruvians kneeling, and prostrate, in all the attitudes of terror and supplication; their wrists and ankles bound by manacles and fetters, the chains of which appear to weigh them down, are, every where, represented in stone-work. The origin of Pizarro, one of the most enterprising and intrepid soldiers, and, at the same time, the most merciless conqueror, whose actions are recorded in the page of modern history, is yet more extraordinary than that of Cortez, In a wood, under the walls of this very city, of which he was afterwards the most wealthy and distinguished noble, he, as a boy, tended swine, and followed for years that mean and humble occupation.

146

CHAPTER 13

Marches & Cantonments

On the 19th, we marched to Jaraicejo, and, on the 20th, to Almaraz. The magnificent scenery for the last two leagues of the road to Almaraz, quite overpowers the mind. You move along a high ridge, and descend gradually from it to the Tagus. On the right, large broken masses of wild, untrodden mountains, clothed in those tints for which there is no name, and which language would in vain describe, bound your view. Far, very far below you, on either side, lie valleys, here verdant with grass, there yellow with corn, and here again, so deep and narrow, that the sun never lights upon their dark and cheerless glens. We crossed the Tagus by a pontoon bridge. The motion of a bridge of this sort, the first time you ever stand on one, is very unpleasant; you stagger, as at sea, and feel quite giddy. We marched over it in files four deep. It is, to be sure, surprising in modern war, to see with what facility an army moves. Is it thought that mountains can impede your march, or that a river can oppose an obstacle? Vain barriers! Cannon are dragged up rocky and precipitous paths, over which no mountain-peasant ever ventured to lead his car; and, in a few hours, a bridge is thrown over a river, before impassable, and a whole army has defiled by it. We now marched by Naval-Moral, and Calzada, to Oropesa, where we halted a few days. To the left of our line of march, the long chain of the lofty Sierra de Avila, its clefts, ravines, and rugged sides, though leagues from you, all, from the clearness and purity of the atmosphere, distinctly visible, invites and rewards your gaze.

Near Naval-Moral we met a Spanish family of rank travelling, a sight very uncommon. The ladies and female attendants were seated in a large heavy, old-fashioned carriage, covered with carved work, and tarnished gilding. This vehicle was drawn by eight mules, which two fine looking men on foot guided, solely by the voice, calling out their names, to which they appeared by their movements to answer with great docility. The gentlemen of the party rode with the male servants, all conversing familiarly together; and these last often put their heads into the carriage-window, and spoke to the ladies. The Spaniards, I have often observed, however exalted their rank, are exceedingly kind and affable to their servants and inferiors. And indeed, the lower classes have much natural politeness; nor is there any thing in their language, or manner, which disgusts or offends. They have no vulgarity in their freedom, nor servility in their respect. I have often sat round the fire of a *posada*, amid Spaniards of all classes, whom chance has assembled together; and have been quite charmed to mark the general good-humour, and the easy, unembarrassed propriety of behaviour of the common peasants. Talavera de la Reyna, where we halted for one night, on the 27th, was, or rather had been, a fine town, famous for its manufactures of silk and porcelain. The country round Talavera is very pleasing; there are many trees and gardens, and a great deal of rich verdure. The memorable and bloody battle of July 28, 1809, was fought near this town; and I walked with a very proud feeling over the left of the position, which our countrymen so bravely and successfully maintained throughout that arduous day. I look upon the battle of Talavera to have been one of the most important that was fought in the Peninsula; and the real and best fruit of which was the gaining of time; time invaluable, and precious beyond all ordinary calculation; for if that battle had not been fought, Portugal would certainly have been invaded a year earlier than it was, and could not have been effectually defended.

There is a wide and excellent road from Talavera to Cevolla, which borders on the Tagus the whole way, and the country you pass through is covered with olive-grounds, and rich, extensive vineyards. At a village where we slept on the 29th, distant about fifteen miles from Toledo, the inhabitants received us with the liveliest demonstrations of joy: we were the first British soldiers they had ever seen, and they treated us with very great hospitality. In the evening, and indeed throughout the night, guitars and castanets were sounding in front of every cottage, and the cheerful peasants gaily testified their joy by dance and song. Their *fandangos* and *seguidillas* are very pleasing; and so long did I linger viewing these happy groups, that the men were already assembling for the march, before I had tasted of repose.

The approach to Toledo, whither we marched in the morning, is fine, and the situation of that interesting city very remarkable. It stands on a conical rock of granite, the base of which is bathed, on two sides, by the Tagus. The appearance of this peninsula, crowded with spires, and turrets, and masses of lofty buildings, when seen at the distance of about three miles, is noble and imposing. We marched into it amid the loud and continued acclamations of a patriotic multitude—were most cordially welcomed, and billeted in the best houses. My host was a rosy-looking canon, who lodged me superbly, and treated me most courteously.

After dressing, and taking a goblet of delicious white wine, I sallied forth to gaze round me, and see all I could before sunset; for with the dawn of day we were again to march forward. The cathedral of Toledo is deservedly the first object of attention with every stranger. I passed three hours in it, but must not attempt a minute description of it. It is upwards of four hundred feet in lengthy and more than two hundred in width. It is built entirely of freestone and marble. Its gates are of bronze, most curiously wrought. The interior of this magnificent temple is richly and splendidly decorated, and corresponds most fully with the noble appearance of its exterior. I speak not, however, of shrines refulgent with gold, and sparkling with jewels; of silver statues, costly plate, and embroidered vestments covered with pearls and precious stones. The treasures and wealth of this cathedral, inferior, perhaps, only to those of the famed Loretto, have disappeared. They have been torn forth by the daring hand of plunder, a circumstance, no one can regret; for they may now, eventually, benefit society, by encouraging industry, and rewarding exertion. I speak of ornaments which still remain, because their removal would have been impossible, and their destruction useless. Of grand monuments, of tombs, screens, and altars adorned with sculpture, or carved with the most delicate and elaborate execution. A fine screen of marble, which is upwards of fifty feet in height, and covered with relief, representing the Ascension, attracts and rivets the attention of every beholder. Many of the best pictures this church could once boast the possession of, have been removed; but in the cloisters are several fine Scripture-paintings by Bayeu, whose designs and colouring are very pleasing.

I heard mass, but was not struck with any thing so grand in the ceremonial, as I had, in such a place, expected. The organ, indeed, was excellent, and the singing good; but had it not been for the noble pile of building above me, I could hardly have supposed the service to be that, at which the primate of all Spain had been wont to assist. The truth, however, was, that the day of the pomp, pride, and power of this cathedral was gone by. Six hundred ecclesiastics once belonged to the service of it, and they were all well provided for. The present number of officiating priests is inconsiderable; nor are they now either powerful or wealthy. The memory of the great and good cardinal Ximenes is greatly venerated in Toledo, and a prayer for his soul is repeated daily at the close of high mass. One word more this venerable church has been built nearly nine hundred years; has been successively possessed by Moors and Christians, and was once surrounded by the habitations of two hundred thousand people, among whom, arts, sciences, and manufactures were busily promoted and encouraged. Of churches, colleges, convents, hospitals, and chapels, upwards of ninety once adorned the streets and squares of this city. It now reckons about six thousand houses, and thirty thousand inhabitants.

I walked from the cathedral to the Alcazar, a palace built on the site of the ancient residence of the Gothic Kings by Charles the Fifth, and long occupied by him. Its grand staircase and spacious gallery, no longer crowded with guards and courtiers, are now dirty, deserted, and silent. This edifice, however, though neglected and decaying, still wears a stately and imposing aspect; and its handsome front, immense quadrangle, and elegant colonnade, declare it to have been the pride and ornament of a happier period. Its situation is very commanding; it stands on the edge of a rocky precipice, nearly perpendicular; at the bottom of which, but full five hundred feet below it, the Tagus flows.

As I toiled through the steep, narrow, inconvenient streets, I never felt one movement of impatience; for the extreme antiquity of this city, gives it an irresistible character of interest; and the *religio loci* always operates most delightfully on the fancy. Hannibal won this spot for Carthage; Romans dwelt in it; Gothic kings reigned in it; Moors have possessed it, and some of the turreted walls still surrounding it were built by them; Spaniards, with their blood, last purchased, and still hold it What a flight for the imagination! to travel back, to conjure up the various scenes acted in the city, and to see sovereigns, warriors, and prelates, whose mouldering dust now sleeps beneath your feet, pass in review before you! So wonderful, however, are the powers of the human mind, that such an indulgence of thought is not only possible, but easy; nor is it denied even to one, who has burst half-educated from the study, and carried with him to the camp little but the imperfect, though fond, recollections of his earlier pursuits.

In the afternoon, I dined with a friend in his billet; and we, who had taken our meals the day before in a cottage chamber not eight feet square, were now seated in an apartment, hung with the richest crimson damask, filled with heavy antique furniture, and, indeed, so gloomily magnificent, as to very greatly interfere with comfort, if not to oppress the spirits.

In the evening we went to the theatre: the play was over, but we were much entertained with a broad, ridiculous farce

151

of two or three scenes, which was acted with some spirit; a boy and girl danced some *boleros* and *fandangos* prettily; but, upon the whole, the amusements hardly repaid you for the annoyance of sitting in a dirty, unadorned, and ill-lighted theatre, and for the poor and wretched appearance of almost all the performers. On leaving the theatre, we bent our steps to the Archbishop's palace, where a ball was given in honour of out arrival. The streets were all illuminated; the façade of the palace, and the dome of the cathedral, most brilliantly and tastefully lighted up, produced a very fine effect. Among the dark sparkling eyes, and olive complexions of the ladies, who were dancing in the ball-room, one girl with light-blue eyes, and exceedingly fair, attracted universal notice. On enquiry I found that she was an orphan, the daughter of Irish parents, who had lived and died in Madrid; and that she had been sent by the government to the *Collegio de Doncellas*, in this city; a very noble institution, where unfortunate young ladies of rank are supported with comfort and elegance; educated with . great liberality, and portioned and given in marriage by the crown. The ball was kept up with great spirit till a late hour, and though I could not venture to join in the waltz, I sat very happily, busied in contemplating the cheerful scene. I felt great interest about the pretty orphan, who I heard, sometimes, attempt a little English to her partner, but with a very foreign accent. How fond such a girl must necessarily become of the husband of her choice;—no bosom to lean upon but his;—no parents, no brothers, no sisters, to claim a share in the generous affections of her youthful heart. Poor girl! I have not forgotten the shades which, at times, even in the lively movements of the dance, stole over your mild countenance; and the purest pleasure I enjoyed that evening was pitying you.

It was very late when I returned to my billet, but I had all the luxury of a short, deep slumber in a capital bed, with sheets of the finest linen, and trimmed with broad muslin borders. In two hours the bugle roused me; in my anti-chamber, neatly laid out on a marble slab, I found chocolate, fruit, and sweet biscuits; and my good canon already up, and waiting to take leave of me. I drank his chocolate, shook him cordially by the hand, mounted, and rode off; and found myself before midday, in a vile, open, unsheltered bivouack, with very little, and very bad water, and not a breath of air stirring around. Such were the varieties, which not unfrequently presented themselves during our marches in the Peninsula. The next day, again brought us into excellent quarters in the small town of Yepes, where we halted for three weeks; during the whole of which period I had the undisturbed possession of three very handsome apartments.

At our entrance into Yepes, a deputation of the principal inhabitants and the clergy, came out to offer a congratulatory address to our general; and in the evening they lighted bonfires and made great rejoicings. This small town is quite surrounded by vineyards, and celebrated for a very delicious white wine. It was the season of the vintage when we arrived; and, for the first week, we saw nothing but cars and mules, laden with baskets of ripe luscious-looking grapes, and surrounded and followed by groups of vintagers of both sexes and all ages, smiling and singing, and looking contented and happy. In this town also, in addition to cheap and plentiful markets, we could procure the finest red wine from Val de Penas; in La Mancha. Long strings of asses, remarkable for their size and beauty, brought this every week, from the interior of the province: and we were enabled, during our stay, to keep tables quite luxurious. Aranjuez, a place well worth visiting, lay within ten miles of us; and as it was within so short a ride, we made frequent excursions to it. Until close to the spot you are little prepared, by the appearance of the surrounding country, for the beautiful vale you are about to descend into. All around, and in front, as far as the eye can reach, plains, not indeed barren, but unadorned with trees, and brown, and parched by the summer and autumnal suns, extend and bound the horizon. Such is the view as you ride towards Aranjuez; but, on a sudden, you find yourself on the very edge of a green valley, filled with groves, and parks, and gardens; and in this enchanting situation, stand the palace and the town.

The palace is not a magnificent building, but a truly comfortable residence, and a rural and shady retreat from the cares and fatigues of royalty. The grounds are extensive, and contain several avenues of lofty and shady elms, nearly three miles in length. The garden round the palace is beautiful, is filled with smaller trees, shrubs, and underwood; and is, perhaps, rather improved to the eye of taste, by having been of late neglected. The *parterres* and the long alleys, have lost much of their formality; and though many of the statues, busts, and fountains, have been broken and defaced, still nature has found a robe to conceal this deformity; for, in many parts, luxuriant ivy and numerous other creepers, have spread, themselves over the ruined fountains, filled the vacant niches, and covered the empty pedestals; and several of the mutilated statues, which are yet standing, are half-coated with a mouling green. All this almost encourages you to fancy that you are walking amid academic groves hallowed by antiquity.

The interior of this palace, like all others, has long suites of apartments, some of which are hung with pictures. The best, are a few of the Flemish and Dutch schools, representing dead game, and subjects of still life; but there are no landscapes or historical pieces at all striking. The chapel, indeed, is adorned with some good paintings in *fresco*, by Bayeu; the same, whose works I saw and admired, in the cloisters of the cathedral at Toledo. Some of the ceilings, too, have fine allegorical paintings, evidently designed and executed by some artist of the Italian school. Some of the chambers in the palace are fitted up in a taste curious, perhaps, but not, I think, pleasing. One, for instance, is entirely panelled with square tiles of China; another with looking-glass. I did not at all admire them. About two miles from the palace stands a building, called Casa del Labrador, erected in 1803, by Charles . the Fourth; and intended as a retreat still more private than the palace. The architecture of this royal farm-house is not fine, though the portico and terrace, ornamented with statues and busts, from the antique, have a handsome appearance; but the interior is fitted up in a style more rich, costly, and elegant, than any thing I ever beheld.

In the vestibule all is marble: the staircase is the finest mahogany. The rooms above are all different, as to the style of their decorations; but all superb. Some are of marble, with the richest gold mouldings; some of the most precious woods beautifully carved and inlaid; some hung with the best modern tapestry; while others are covered with landscapes, delicately and curiously wrought in needlework, I was more struck myself with the richness and variety of the marbles, (all of which were from different provinces in Spain,) than with the more costly and valuable ornaments. However, for my part, I was not sorry to quit the spot; for you grow fatigued and restless with gazing on the dazzling splendour of such apartments. My companion was envying the possession of this voluptuous residence, till I reminded him, that the late owner had met with infidelity in his queen, ingratitude in his son, treason in his counsellors, and contempt among his people; and that while we were ranging, without care or fear, through these peaceful groves, the miserable Charles was dwelling in captivity beyond the Appenines.

We returned through the town; it is modern, and regularly built at right angles; the streets are wide and spacious, some adorned with fountains, and some of them having a double row of trees in the centre; the houses, too, are very uniform; most of them are white, and have their window-shutters painted green. We entered one large magnificent house, which had formerly been the habitation of a grandee, but was now filled with soldiers. The ceilings and sides of the large spacious apartments, in which they lay, were all painted elegantly in *fresco*. How little did the mistress of this stately mansion suppose, that, within so short a period, her company saloons, so often filled with youth, and beauty, and fashion, and unsuspecting pride, would be converted, by the fate of war, into barracks. These revolutions in the common order of things are strange; but to none do they appear so strange as to an Englishman, who, throughout his whole life, never distantly contemplates the possibility of being driven from the shelter of his own roof. The present dullness and desertion of Aranjuez is felt the more, from the modern and gay style of its buildings, and from the recollection, that it was not very long ago a place of the most fashionable resort, and filled, during the summer, with nobles and courtiers.

The situation of public affairs did not long permit us to remain quiet in our excellent cantonments. In the north, Burgos, very successfully resisted all attempts to reduce it; and the army under Clausel, which had taken shelter behind the Ebro, began to recover strength and confidence, and to menace such of our forces as were covering or conducting the operations against that fortress. On our side, Soult, who had effected his junction with Joseph Buonaparte, at Almanza, on the borders of Valencia, was advancing with powerful forces to Madrid, while Ballasteros, who might have rendered the most important services by harassing Soult on his route, and uniting his people to ours on the Tagus, obstinately halted in Grenada. Ballasteros was a man who wanted neither courage nor ability; but his silly pride would not allow him to receive the orders of Wellington; and, by his ridiculous vanity, the cause was very much injured at a most critical moment, and it became impossible for us to maintain ourselves in the heart of Spain, or to defend Madrid.

On the night of the 22nd of October, our brigade marched from Yepes to Aranjuez: on the 26th we crossed the Tagus, and manoeuvred until the 30th on that river and the Jarama. An attempt was made by the enemy on the 30th to possess themselves of the Puente-larga, on the Jarama river; they were, however, repulsed by a British brigade, under Colonel Skerret, with a trifling loss on both sides.

CHAPTER 14

Brushes With the Enemy

In the night of the 30th we commenced our retreat; and at nine o'clock in the morning of the 31st our columns were passing under the walls of Madrid. This city I had never seen, and orders were very properly, but provokingly issued, that no one should be allowed to leave the columns, and no one, on any account, be permitted to enter the city. I was literally burning with curiosity, and would almost have faced a volley of musketry to see Madrid; in fact, I am a friend to discipline, but I could not resist I stole from the column, made my way over a bridge, and passed half an hour in riding through the streets and squares. Only half an hour!—What could you, exclaims my reader, what could you see in the time? Why I saw the new palace, a most noble building, which has immortalised its architect Sacchetti. It is quadrangular in its form—each front 470 feet in length, and 100 in height, from base to cornice, with a most elegant balustrade above; it certainly yields the palm to no edifice it has fallen to my lot to see, but the Louvre. I went slowly down the Calla-ancha, a wide, handsome, and magnificent street. I looked into the Prado, stood under the Puerto d'Alcala, a gate, or barrier of the city, the central arch of which is seventy feet in height. I alighted in the grand square, and had coffee served to me in a large saloon, filled with the gentlemen of Madrid. One of them, approaching me, said, with tears in his eyes, "I know the English are brave, and loyal—I know this retreat is a measure of necessity; but why, why did you come hither, if you could not calculate on maintaining possession? You little know the misery and terror which at this moment fill the bosoms of the inhabitants of this city. A few hours may deliver them up to the vengeance of Spain's deadly enemies, and the disaffected traitors within these walls have watched us well: they will represent every act of loyalty as a crime, every *viva* as a cry of insurrection against the odious government of Joseph."

My heart quite sunk within me, as he spoke; I could only reply, that the policy of the French would never suffer them to punish offences so general; that they would feel their own stay uncertain, and must calculate on our return at some future period; that this mortifying abandonment of the capital was never contemplated when we advanced, and, even now, was only rendered necessary by the folly of their own country-man, Ballasteros. He pressed my hand, uttered a *"viva mil annos"* as I mounted my horse, and I was soon out of his sight.

The people, though dreadfully dejected, showed no signs of anger or indignation, but were respectful and friendly to the last. I led the city, encountered no general to put me under an arrest, a punishment I am free to confess I deserved, and reached the camp highly delighted at having seen Madrid; for, after all, is it not possible to see in one half hour a scene of interest which may be remembered for ever? I would certainly have given much to have examined Madrid at my leisure; but for the general effect of the superb palace, the streets, the squares, the outward picture of that city, I have seen, admired them, and can speak, as to the impression produced, as well as a man who has passed weeks there as a resident.

Our bivouack, on the evening of the first of November, commanded a clear but distant view of the town and palace of Escurial. Though within two leagues of us, I could not visit them; but I was well reconciled to this disappointment, for I examined the palace attentively with my glass, and could discover that the royal residence, and the convent attached to it, formed a shapeless, and frightful pile of building.

What, indeed, could be expected, when a whimsical monarch

commanded his architect to take a gridiron for his model, and in the erection of the edifice, and the disposition of its various parts, to conform most strictly to this strange plan? The convent of San Lorenzo was, in its day, exceedingly wealthy, and could once boast a valuable library of thirty thousand volumes, and a very fine collection of paintings, among which were several masterpieces of the famous Titian: this celebrated and exquisite painter resided for upwards of five years in Spain, and left many precious works behind him. Indeed, at one period of her history, Spain, from her intimate connection with Italy, was not only embellished by the labours of Italian architects, but the saloons of her kings and nobles were furnished with many a rich production of the Italian pencil. The names of Michael Angelo, Raphael, Guido, Leonardo da Vinci, and the Caraccis, were well known in Madrid, while the works of Murillo, and other natives of Spain, attest, that there was a time when the divine art of painting met with honour and encouragement among Spaniards of rank and affluence.

On the 2nd of November, after a delightful march through a romantic country, we took up our ground at the foot of the Guadarama pass; on the following morning we ascended these rude[16] mountains, and moved upon Villa Castin. The ascent to the top of the pass is four miles, but the royal road is so fine, and so admirably laid down, that your cannon meet with no obstacle, which an additional pair of horses, or a drag-rope cannot overcome. The descent into the plains of old Castile is not less than eight miles, and eight more bring you to Villa Castin. Descriptions of scenery are, at best, but feeble, for to describe material objects with the pen is difficult, if not impossible. I shall therefore content myself with saying, that the southern face of the Guadarama mountains is bare, brown, and rocky, but the northern side most majestically wild; large projecting masses of rock, dark, and thick plantations of the mountain fir; tumbling torrents, and steep patches of the liveliest verdure, all boldly blended, are the features of this grand and uncommon scene.

16. The most elevated points of the Sierra de Guadarama are eight thousand feet above the level of the sea.

Our march this day was rendered still more interesting by the distinct view, which, from the top of the pass, you enjoyed of the various columns, defiling by the beautifully winding road, on which not less than thirty thousand men might be seen in motion. The plains of old Castile are very extensive, and their extreme flatness is fatiguing to the eye, but they are in general well cultivated, and filled with towns and villages. We traversed them rapidly. On the 5th we were in communication with Lord Wellington, who had broken up from before Burgos, and was retiring on Salamanca, followed by Clausel.

On the 6th we halted, for one day, on the heights of Canta-racilla, reached Alba de Tormes on the evening of the seventh, and the whole of the allies were posted on the eighth in and near Salamanca, and along the line of the Tormes, occupying the town of Alba on the right, with some British, and a division of Portuguese. The French armies of the north, south, and centre, which had followed us from Burgos on the one side, and Madrid on the other, successively arrived in our front; and it was generally thought that Lord Wellington would try the fate of a battle. On the 10th, a column of infantry, with cannon, attacked the town and castle of Alba; it was repulsed. On the 14th, Soult, who commanded for Joseph, caused an immense force to pass the Tormes above Alba. Our division immediately fell back, on its right, from that neighbourhood, and drew nearer Salamanca. From a high rocky ridge, behind which our division was formed in contiguous close columns, we saw the enemy's infantry, occupying a low wooded height, about a mile from us. They showed about five thousand of their horse on the plain below us, while on that to our rear, the whole of our cavalry was formed and ready to act. There was some skirmishing and cannonading, but no affair of moment.

On the fifteenth, at daylight, the whole of our army was in order of battle; our division was posted behind the Arripeles, and every one anticipated a fierce and general engagement. The French had ninety thousand men, and nearly two hundred pieces of artillery. Our division had not been present at the glorious victory of Salamanca, and longed eagerly for the battle; for they naturally thought that a brilliant and successful contest, on a much grander scale, and on the same ground, would give them a right to speak, of the field of Salamanca with a soldier's pride. This jealousy of fame, this "avarice of praise," is common in camps; and I need hardly add, incalculably useful to sovereigns and commanders-in-chief. Soult, however, had no intention of fighting; he declined the challenge, manoeuvred on our right, and threatening our communication with Portugal, compelled us to retreat. It is evident that Lord Wellington, who, from the 8th to the 15th, kept all his forces concentrated on the Tormes, anxiously desired and expected a general engagement. Indeed, it has been said, and is probable, that on the morning of the 15th, could he, have supposed that Soult would refuse fighting, he would himself have been the assailant, and have marched boldly on the heights of Mozarbes. It was not until ten o'clock in the forenoon that the retreat was ordered, which, had it been the original intention of his Lordship, would, no doubt, have been entered upon six hours earlier. About two in the afternoon, our column, having moved by its right, arrived on the high road to Ciudad Rodrigo, and marched towards the Agueda. About noon, on this day, the rain began to fall in torrents, wetting us to the skin, yet not being without its use, for it most admirably masked our movements.

I have, in the course of these pages, often painted the bivouack as a scene of enjoyment and pleasure, and many will accuse me of exaggeration; but I have spoken as I felt, and I can truly declare that, in nine cases out of ten, we enjoy rather than suffer. But it is not to be denied, that we occasionally endure what a person, unacquainted with service, can ill conceive, and would with difficulty, be persuaded to credit. From the 15th to the evening of the 19th, our sufferings were of this description. On our march we were deluged with rain, the roads were deep and miry, and we had repeatedly to ford rivers and streams, some of which were breast high. In our bivouacs the ground was soaked, no dry wood to be had, and our fires, if any, were smoky and cheerless. In addition to this we were miserably provided, having neither bread, biscuit, nor flour.[17] Lean bullocks, which travelled with us, were slaughtered daily as we halted, and putting your miserable ration on a stick, or the point of your, sword, you broiled it on wood-ashes, and ate it greedily, half-smoked, and half-raw, without knife, fork, or any conveniences, the whole of our baggage having, of course, preceded us. On the 16th, indeed, my regiment was posted as a picquet on a small plateau, just above the village of Matilla, and we certainly had some prospect of comparative comfort.

In this hamlet, though there was no bread, we luckily found a few potatoes, which having eagerly purchased, we were boiling at a tolerable fire, in a mean hovel, and chuckling at our good fortune, when the sound of a few shots caused us to run out, and we found about two squadrons of our German Hussars retiring before a large body of the enemy's horse. As we had only piled arms in column at quarter distance, we were instantaneously formed, and the enemy halted about musket-shot from us. We stood, for about fifteen minutes, calmly looking at each other. They were about two thousand in number, all covered with large white cloaks, and looked remarkably well. It certainly was a sight, which, on any ordinary occasion, it would have been worth losing a dinner for; but hungry and exhausted as we were, the bustle they caused was very unseasonable. They suffered us to retire through the village, and across the plain to the wood, where our division lay, unmolested; for as they had no guns, it would have been a ticklish affair to attempt any thing against a steady battalion of infantry; but they pushed down about six squadrons to

---

17. Such was the scarcity of bread, that a friend of mine, a paymaster, who lost our column, and was wandering for two days on another road, overtook a Spanish peasant, who was journeying with his wife and children towards Ciudad Rodrigo, and seeing a loaf of bread on the mule he was leading, he begged to purchase it, but the man refused to sell it. Faint and almost wild with hunger, he pulled out a *doubloon*, and offered it as the price of the loaf, but the man still declined, saying, pithily, "My little ones cannot eat gold." What a lesson for the pampered citizen, who thinks there is nothing gold cannot buy!

the left of the village, and had a trifling brush with some of our. cavalry, who came up hastily from their camp, after which they retired, and occupied for the night Matilla and the heights.

In our bivouack on the 17th, a cannonade, directed against the right column, and very distant from us, caused us to stand to our arms shivering for two hours, after which we broiled our ration, and lay down in a swamp, nearly ankle-deep in water, to repose. This same day, Sir Edward Paget, our second in command, was taken, while quietly riding in an interval between two divisions, one of which was marching in his rear. A few Polish lancers had adventurously straggled through the wood on our flank, and coming down upon the road, carried him off through the forest undiscovered.

On the night of the 18th the rain ceased for a short time, but just as we were composing ourselves for sleep, a handful of Indian corn was issued to each man, and they all immediately began pounding it between large stones, which strange handmills they passed from one to the other, keeping up such a noise throughout the whole night, that no one in camp could possibly have closed his eyes. Such were the little additions to our annoyance and misery. The sufferings of mind, however, on a retreat, are far less endurable than privation and fatigue: these last, animated by the hopes which a forward movement never fails to inspire, we cheerfully bear; but it is distressing to feel, that if you drop, from inanition and exhaustion, you fall an easy and unresisting prey to the enemy; The loss of our army on this retreat was very considerable, fully equal to the casualties of a general action, and thanks to the supineness of the French, who never vigorously pushed us, that it was not doubled.

On the night of the 20th, our corps of the army was distributed in mountain villages, south of the Sierra de Francia, and here we halted for eight days. Here, too, we were restored to our baggage, and under cover. Miserable as were the hovels in which we were quartered, our gaiety in these chimney-corners, where we sat roasting chestnuts, arid boiling potatoes, would not a little have surprised our friends at home, could they by magic have been transported from their curtained and carpeted drawing-rooms to these mountain-cots, and have seen the accommodation we thought ourselves so fortunate in procuring.

On the 28th, the whole of Hill's corps marched for the province of Coria. Our route lay through that mountainous region, which divides the Partido de Ciudad Rodrigo from that of Alcantara, in Estremadura. The scenery, as is ever the case in such a country, was truly magnificent: the passage of the rude and lofty Sierra de Gata, and the descent from the top of the pass to the town, abound with subjects for the pencil of a Salvator Rosa. A rugged and dangerous road winds amid the thickest brushwood, and around the boldest rocks; below it, on one side, are precipices the most frightful, while, above, on the other, huge masses of mountain-stone terrifically impend, and seem to threaten the traveller with instant destruction. We were very fortunate in our day; and saw this country to great advantage. In the very loftiest regions of the Sierra, a veil of mist enveloped us, which, as we descended, gradually cleared away, and gave to our view plains, and woods, and villages, all lighted by a glorious sun, and smiling as in summer. The little town of Gata lies immediately at the foot of these mountains, most romantically situated, and half-concealed by thick groves of chestnut trees, which grow there to a handsome and prodigious size, are found in great abundance, and whose chestnuts are indeed the principal food of the poorer inhabitants. The march, to a man of any mind or feeling, always presents enjoyment, especially when it lies among mountains, those grand features of scenery, which are, throughout romantic Spain, thrown everywhere by the bold hand of nature in the richest and wildest profusion.

My regiment lay at a small village in the neighbourhood of Coria, from November to the middle of May. When settled in our winter quarters, Lord Wellington addressed a sweeping and angry circular to the troops, reproaching them with having displayed a greater want of discipline on their retreat "than any army with which," said his Lordship, "I have ever served, or of which: I have ever read." In this same circular, the men were told that they had

164

suffered; no privation which could justify the least irregularity, or account for the losses which had been sustained, and they were bitterly reproached for riot cooking with the same expedition as the French soldiery. As to the first charge, I am confident that his Lordship was never made acquainted with the extent of their privations; and for the latter, most satisfactory reasons might have been given for our comparative tardiness in preparing our food. The French soldiers mess by twos and threes, and have small kettles; the English, at that time, had large camp-kettles of iron, one to every ten men. The French took wood of all sorts, and wherever they found it; our orders, on this head, were properly, but particularly strict. Neither were the irregularities, though great, by any means general: there were corps, and many corps, who maintained their discipline, and whose casualties were comparatively trifling, and most satisfactorily accounted for. I believe the interior economy of British regiments, and the discipline of a British company, in a regiment well commanded, to be superior to that of any army in the world, and sure I am, that the Duke of Wellington, who, since that period, has served with some, and seen troops of all the other armies in Europe, is now of the same opinion. The army felt all this deeply, though they made every allowance for the severe disappointment which the failure before Burgos, and the loss of ground in the heart of Spain, must have naturally produced in the bosom of that commander through whose ability and valour, their situation in the foregoing August had been rendered so transcendently brilliant.

Coria, the head quarters of Sir Rowland Hill throughout the winter from 1812 to 13, is a small town of about 600 houses, prettily situated on the river Alagon; has a cathedral, and is further adorned by the fine remains of a Moorish tower and castle. Wherever you move in Spain, the vestiges of these warlike Moors are to be traced. It is strange that more is not known, among us, about the state of Spain, under their dominion, for they were certainly a civilized and polished people, and introduced many arts and sciences among the natives of Spain, which, till their arrival, were unknown: they had knowledge of agriculture, skill and taste in architecture; had their learned men, poets, and men of science, and from what we know of the costliness of their dress and arms, must have had precious and flourishing manufactures.

Even as late as the beginning of the sixteenth century, a million of Moriscoes, who doubtless, if they did not retain the dress, customs, and manners of their ancestors, had many cherished traditions concerning their greatness and their history, still dwelt in Spain; yet nothing is known. I should anxiously have desired to visit those provinces in the south, which the Moors so long occupied, and where they have left behind them such noble memorials, as the Alhambra of Grenada, the Mosque of Cordova, and other magnificent ruins found south of the Sierra Morena. Cheerfully would I thus have employed my winter leisure, but a military man is spared the trouble of exercising his will in these matters. I therefore remained, like others, quiet under the roof of an honest peasant, and!made myself as contented as I could. In the neighbourhood of pur cantonment, the Alagon, a river, whose waters were more .beautifully clear than any I ever beheld; pursued its tranquil course; behind us rose some rocky heights, well wooded, where the walks were exceedingly pretty, and many leagues in our front, the eye might ever seek, and rest upon the stupendous mountains of Bejar, covered with eternal snow.

Many as were the weeks we passed in the same small village, I never looked upon that finely formed Sierra, but with a feeling that almost repressed the wish to wander. The season too of winter is in that province mild as an English spring; our tables were well supplied with game and wine: we had books and newspapers; these last contained long details of the Russian campaign, and were therefore highly interesting. To be sure, in such a situation, a sigh for the fireside, the evening concert, the ball, the play, the well remembered gaieties of England, will intrude; yet how many were the social evenings, how many the happy hours of rational and lively converse, which I enjoyed in that quiet village, with men, whom death, wounds, and distant service have now torn from my side.

Rapidly did time glide by till spring again returned, and brought with it new hopes, and the prospect of another interesting campaign. Every effort had been made, during our long halt, to render the various corps efficient in discipline, field exercise, and equipment An order of Lord Wellington's directed, that three tents per company should be carried for the men, on the bat mules, hitherto appropriated to the conveyance of the large iron camp kettles, the use of which was discontinued, and small ones substituted, to be carried by the soldiers themselves,

The twentieth of May found us again in the field, bivouacked at the foot of the Puerto de Baños, through which, a better road than that of Gata runs from Plasencia to Salamanca. The sun was shining fiercely upon our tents in the vale, while immediately above us, at an immense elevation, rose the snowy and frozen peaks of the Sierra de Bejar. The following morning we climbed the pass; the ascent commences at Baños, a small town, very poor, and in ruins, having been plundered, and half destroyed by a corps of the French in 1809. It is famous for a remarkably fine natural hot bath, and was it not seated in so wild and rude a country, would doubtless have been much frequented by invalids. We halted, for one night, at the very top of the pass; the march down into Castile is romantic and beautiful in the extreme; below, meadows clothed with the richest verdure, watered with innumerable streams, and enclosed with hedgerows, as in England, promise you delightful situations for encamping; and, ever as you raise your eye to the right, and above you, are majestic mountains covered with eternal snow; and at the rising and setting of the sun, all bright and varying with hues and tints of the most heavenly dye.

We traversed a very interesting country to Salamanca, where we arrived on the twenty-sixth: the enemy's rear-guard, consisting of 400 cavalry, 3000 infantry, and four guns, evacuated the town as we approached. We did not march into the city, but forded the Tormes a mile to the right of it The French fired a few shots at our leading brigade of cavalry as it formed after passing the river, and then rapidly retired along the Tormes towards Babila Fuente. They were pursued, cannonaded, and much pressed by our cavalry, and horse artillery, and sustained a loss of about 200 killed and wounded, and as many taken. We were, this day, in communication with the column which marched under the order of Wellington, who was himself present at the affair with the enemy's rear-guard.

There is scarcely a place in all Spain, the name of which is so familiar to our ears as Salamanca. Le Sage, in his admirable Gil Blas, has immortalized it, and we all feel acquainted with the students of Salamanca; but we looked for them in vain, as we walked under the handsome stone *piazza* of the most noble looking square in Spain. These were, indeed, filled with a motley crowd of people, but we could discern no youthful scholars in their academic habits; many thousands once studied in this university. A few, with some of the old professors, still lingered in; the deserted colleges, or might be seen pacing in the spacious aisles of the elegant cathedral. But war spares neither the abode of piety, nor the seat of learning; numbers of the students, at an early period of the war, obeyed the sacred call of their country, and left their peaceful colleges for the tumultuous camp. In the year 1812, two convents in Salamanca were fortified and garrisoned by the French, besieged and taken by the British; thus, an open and quiet city became a scene of contest, confusion, and blood-shed. Monks yielded up their cells to soldiers; all the houses for a certain space round these convents were razed; while the more distant were injured, and beat down by the heavy fire of the French batteries, and many of the streets and lanes were enfiladed by their cannon; heaps of ruins every where presented themselves to my sight; and, tired of gazing on poor Salamanca in such a state of degradation, I returned to my tent and my blanket.

On our line of march, the following morning, the British and Portuguese divisions of infantry, in the corps of Sir Rowland Hill, passed Lord Wellington in review; we had upwards of 14,000 bayonets, and made a very fine appearance. There is something very pleasing to real soldiers in being reviewed in this ready convenient manner, without fuss or preparation, and to a general there must be something, I think, gratifying in looking at his men all rough and dusty with the march, even as they would go into battle.

Our division encamped the same evening in a wood, near Orbada, about sixteen miles in front of Salamanca; here, and distributed in the neighbourhood, the right wing of the army halted, while the left, in pursuance of Wellington's able disposition, was gaining the enemy's right by the route of Miranda and Carvajales. On the third of June, we we were again in motion, and, on the fourth we passed the Douro, near Toro, without opposition, for the enemy, out-manoeuvred and alarmed, was compelled to abandon the line of that river, without an effort, and hastily retired, destroying the bridges; that at Toro we repaired with a temporary platform, and our infantry crossed it by files; the cavalry, artillery, and baggage passing at a ford about a quarter of a mile above the town. Toro is a fine handsome old city, and is adorned with a very large and beautiful tower of Moorish construction, in the highest preservation; there are also convenient public walks all round the walls, thickly planted with trees. We bivouacked for the night, in a good pine wood, near the village of Morales, and close to the ground where the day previous our hussars had had a very brilliant affair with a superior body of French heavy dragoons, sabring great numbers, and taking about two hundred prisoners. We continued our march across the fertile plains of the province of Valladolid; on the sixth we saw that city, at a distance, and halted within two leagues of it on the seventh, but I had no opportunity of visiting it; on the eighth we took up our ground near a ruined village; out of two hundred houses only ten remained habitable. There was a church in this place, which had been most curiously and ingeniously fortified by the French, as a post for a detachment; platforms were constructed here for all their sentries, so raised and protected, as to secure them from surprise: such was the state of watchfulness and preparation, which, even amid the plains occupied by their armies, traversed by their columns, and scoured by their cavalry, all the small detachments of the enemy were compelled most strictly to observe. These things are proofs of the resistance of the Spanish nation, and the active hatred of the people; for if such was the situation of the enemy, in the very plains, where discipline may, and often does most success-fully oppose both courage and numbers, what must it have been amid the more mountainous districts, abounding in fastnesses, and rocky passes, known to, and tenable by, a brave and patriotic peasantry. The Guerilla system had certainly a most powerful, a most material influence in the salvation of Spain. May the same system, acted upon by the ablest *partisans* among the "*Liberales*," again save her from the worst, the most formidable of enemies, a domestic tyrant, a monarch who may have the right to govern, but not the right to oppress her.

CHAPTER 15

The Battle of Vittoria

It was not until the 12th that we saw the enemy, and so clean-
ly had they retreated, that we had met with no stragglers, and
since the affair of cavalry at Toro, had taken no prisoners. Our
march and movements on the 12th were rather interesting. Sir
Rowland Hill's corps broke up from Manzana at five o'clock in
the morning, and moved forwards in two columns, the right on
Celada, the left, in which I was, on Hornillo, through Juntana.
The enemy skirmished very prettily with our cavalry at Hormasa, a small village, on a river of that name, and made a short
stand to favour the retreat of the main body of their rear guard;
they then retired slowly up the heights, above Hornillo, whither
we followed them. They had at Hormasa about four squadrons
and three battalions. Their infantry formed line on these heights,
and, as we ascended on their flank, threw it back, changing its
direction, but still presenting us a front. At last, perceiving that
we were in great strength, and had large bodies of cavalry up,
they threw themselves into squares, and retiring over the river Arlanzon, joined the remainder of the French corps under
Count Reille, and the whole took the road to Burgos. These
troops manoeuvred very rapidly and steadily; and effected their
retreat in most beautiful order, in the face of our cavalry, and
under the fire of some of our artillery, which, however, did very
little execution. At the close of this affair, I had the gratification
of seeing on these heights nearly the whole of the British cavalry. Most of the brigades passed us in columns of half squadrons,

as they were returning to take up their ground for the night. The masses of heavy dragoons, with their brazen helmets, horse-hair plumes, and long crimson cloaks, had a most superb and martial appearance; and were happily contrasted by the light, ready, and active look of the hussars, whose equipment and dress were neat and becoming.

Our infantry columns returned also, and encamped on the line of the Hormasa river, leaving strong picquets on the heights. One of these picquets I commanded; it began to rain heavily towards the evening, and poured for several hours. To add to our comfort we had nothing to eat, and on these bare hills there was no wood for firing. The morning, however, brought with it consolation; for, at early dawn, while gazing with my glass at the distant castle of Burgos, I had the satisfaction to see it suddenly enveloped in thick white smoke, and the sound of a tremendous explosion announced to me that the enemy had blown up, and would of course abandon it. In ten minutes a second explosion followed, and, in about a quarter of an hour, I could distinctly see the yawning ruins.

A very large French army was now collected on the Ebro; for Joseph, with all the troops who had been at Madrid, Segovia, &c. had marched rapidly by the pass of Somosierra, on Avanda and Burgos, and were now moving in front of us. Although there was no longer a Burgos to besiege or blockade, to have forced the pass of Pancorro, and have crossed the Ebro at Miranda had been impossible. Wellington moved as rapidly by the left, on an unfrequented road, and passing the Ebro by the Fuente de Arenas, marched directly on Vittoria, whither the enemy retired. Our column moved on the evening of the 13th to Villorejo. The road lay through a very pretty valley, filled with small, neat-looking villages: corn and meadow land, poplars and willows, gave it quite an English character. On the whole of the 15th, as we traversed the plain to Villascusa, we had a fine distinct view of the sierras of Asturias on our left.

On the 16th, we descended by a steep and rocky road into a low secluded valley, through which the Ebro, here narrow and inconsiderable, winds its way,, and crossing the river by a stone bridge of five arches, turned to the left, and followed a road running, for nearly two miles, along the bank of the Ebro, and almost on a level with its waters. The view of this valley, on your descent to it, the vale itself, and the singularly picturesque road by which you pass out from it, are among the most, enchanting scenes it has ever fallen to my lot to contemplate. Here you may imagine yourself transported to the happy retreat described in Rasselas. On every side mountains enclose and shelter this favoured spot; all the passes leading to and from it are concealed from you; the fields all teem with cultivation, and the orchards all blush with fruit: the ash, the beech, and the poplar, the woodbine, the rose, and a thousand shrubs, shade and adorn the rural dwellings. The narrow wheel-track, by which you leave this elysium, runs curving at the foot of impending precipices, so bold and varied in their forms, and the character of their beauties, that no pen could describe them justly. Here they are clothed with rich and shaggy brushwood, there naked to their blue or grey summits, which frown above you; and here, again, from the rude clefts and fissures of the rock, grow solitary trees and plants, where no hand can ever reach them, while, in some places, thick wreaths of ivy half cover the projecting crags. The river brawls along between these cliffs, often impeded by huge masses of mountain stone, which have fallen in some wintry storm, or been detached by some violent convulsion of nature, and now form islands in its bed. In a scene so lovely, soldiers seemed quite misplaced, and the glittering of arms, the trampling of horses, and the loud voices of the men, appeared to insult its peacefulness. On the three following days our bivouacs were delightful; fine wood and water, and grand scenery, all combined to make us cheerful and contented.

At half past seven on the morning of the 21st, our column entered the high road running from Miranda to Vittoria, and marching through the small town of Puebla, amid the *vivas* of the inhabitants, with our music playing and colours flying, we, in half an hour more, halted in the presence of the French army, which was formed in order of battle, on a position of great strength. Their right was stationed near the city of Vittoria, their centre commanded the valley of the Zadorra, and their left rested on the lofty heights which rise above Puebla.[18] The battle array of a large army is a most noble and imposing sight. To see the hostile lines and columns formed, and prepared for action; to observe their generals and mounted officers riding smartly from point to point, and to mark every now and then, one of their guns opening on your own staff, reconnoitring them, is a scene very animating, and a fine prelude to a general engagement.

On your own side, too, the hammering of flints and loosening of cartridges; the rattle of guns and tumbrils, as they come careering up to take their appointed stations; and the swift galloping of *aid-de-camps* in every direction, here bringing reports to their generals, there conveying orders to the attacking columns, all speak of peril and death, but also of anticipated victory; and so cheeringly, that a sensation of proud hope swells the bosom, which is equal, if not superior, to the feeling of exultation in the secure moment of pursuit and triumph. With the exception of the sixth, which was detained at Medina, all the divisions of the Anglo-Portuguese army, and those of the Spanish under the orders of Giron, Longa, and Murillo, were present in this field. We could not have had less than 74,000 men, and the French about 60,000, with a numerous artillery.

The corps of Sir Rowland Hill, in pursuance of the general arrangements, began the action by attacking the enemy's left. From the moment that we passed Puebla, a Spanish brigade, under the orders of General Murillo, was sent up the heights, rising above that town, and was afterwards supported by the 71st Regiment, some light companies, and a battalion of Portuguese caçadores, all commanded by the Honourable Colonel Cadogan, of the 71st. These troops were heavily engaged long before the action became general, and sustained great loss; but,

---

18. On a very steep and commanding height on the right of the enemy's centre, flew a white standard, said to mark the head-quarters and the presence of Joseph Bonaparte.

at length, succeeded in gaining possession of these important heights, and in dislodging and driving down the enemy. My brigade marched upon the village of Subijana de Alava, in front of the line, and had orders to carry it with the bayonet. The enemy opened upon us with fourteen pieces of artillery, from their position, as we moved down, but with little effect. I could never persuade myself that they would resign so important a post as the village without a struggle; and when we got close to it, and began to find the ground difficult and intersected with walls and banks, I expected every moment to be saluted with a murderous discharge of musketry, and to see them issue forth; and I had prepared my men to look for, and disregard such an attack.

Not a soul, however, was in the village; but a wood a few hundred yards to its left, and the ravines above it, were filled with French light infantry, I, with my company, was soon engaged in smart skirmishing among the ravines, and lost about eleven men, killed and wounded, out of thirty-eight. The English do not skirmish so well as the Germans or the French; and it really is hard work to make them preserve their proper extended order, cover themselves, and not throw away their fire; and in the performance of this duty, an officer is, I think, far more exposed than in line-fighting. I enjoyed, however, from my elevated post, a very fine view of the field. Below me, it was really dreadful to see how the other regiments, which skirmished opposite the wood, suffered from the fire of the French voltigeurs. It was about two o'clock when the fourth and light divisions crossed the Zadorra, by a bridge opposite Nanclares, deployed, and advanced boldly against the enemy's centre and town of Ariñez. About the same hour, the third and seventh divisions forced the bridge of the Puentes, and attacked, and drove his right. All this time there was a tremendous fire of artillery on both sides; but, as this slackened, the enemy was seen preparing to retire; and he soon abandoned every village, height, and position, in great confusion. We marched rapidly in pursuit, but to little purpose; and halted in the evening in a bivouack about two miles in front, and to the right of Vittoria.

Here, news about the general result of the battle came pouring in every moment; and we found, that the enemy, having been cut off from the Bayonne road by Sir Thomas Graham, (who, with the British and Spanish divisions under his orders, had dislodged him, after a sharp conflict, from Gamarra Mayor, and Abechuco,) had fled in the direction of Pampeluna, abandoning the whole of his baggage and artillery. One hundred and fifty pieces of cannon, 415 caissons, their military chest, and upwards of 3000 carriages, wagons, and cars, laden with stores, treasure, and plunder, had fallen into our hands. Our loss had been about 5000 killed and wounded; and that of the French not more considerable, I confess, I was disappointed with the result, and had looked for more solid, and less high sounding advantages. It is true, the capture of all their artillery and materiel was a brilliant triumph; and in those days when generals would have sacrificed an army for their preservation, would have been regarded with wonder and admiration. For my part, I would much sooner have heard of heavy casualties in the French ranks, and have seen a good solid column of them prisoners. I was smiled at, and called unreasonable; but this very army, deprived of its artillery, stript of its baggage, and driven into France in twelve days after the victory, in eighteen more resumed the offensive, assaulted our positions in the passes of the Pyrenees, penetrated to within a league of Pampeluna, and fought a battle for its relief. After all, however, when I reflect, that our army was brought, in five and forty days, from the frontiers of Portugal to the confines of France, a distance of 400 miles; and that a powerful enemy was driven before us, through the defiles of the lower Pyrenees, I am lost in admiration of the talent of Wellington; and should, perhaps, feel ashamed to own my disappointment on the field of Vittoria.

In this battle, one regiment of our division, the 71st, suffered severely, losing 400 men, and their gallant commander, the Hon. Colonel Cadogan. This brave officer, it is reported, mortally wounded, and fully aware of his situation, begged to be carried to a higher point than that on which he fell, that he might see how the battle went, and gaze to the last on the advance of our victorious troops. This trait of patriotism would have figured well in Greek or Roman story; as it is, it remains a camp anecdote, related or listened to with pleasure, but without wonder, by men, who have seen, common British soldiers, covered with wounds, expire in the very act of cheering. I am one, who suspect, that three hundred British grenadiers would have held the pass of Thermopylæ as stoutly as the Spartans; and have considered it as the simple discharge of a perilous and important duty, to die on the ground on which they fought. Not that I think less highly of the ancients; but only as highly of the moderns. Insensible to a tale of heroism I can never feel; and I admit, that such a tale is ever hallowed by the remoteness of the age in which the action it relates has been performed; but I condemn those who rave about Greeks and Romans; and because division and regiment do not sound quite so classical as legion and cohort, would persuade us, that musketeers are not as brave as *hastati*; or British captains worthy to be classed with Roman centurions.

On the morning of the 22nd, the army marched forwards, leaving a captain's detachment from every regiment in Vittoria, I was sent on this unpleasant duty. The streets of the town, as may be imagined, were all bustle and confusion: here, cars, filled indiscriminately with French, English, and Portuguese wounded, were conveying their groaning burthens to the convents allotted for their hospitals. There, officers wounded and pale, their uniforms all bloodstained and dirty, were riding towards their billets at a slow pace; their servants leading the animals by the bridle, and often supporting their drooping and suffering masters, to whom the agony of motion appeared intolerable. Here, a few groups of French prisoners stood, eagerly looking out from the door of the church where they were confined; there, our detachments lay halted in the streets, waiting for orders; while long trains of commissariat mules laden with biscuit, were filing past us to follow the army. From the gate, Spanish troops were marching in to garrison Vittoria, while astonishment was painted on the features of the inhabitants; to whom, having been so long under the dominion of the French, their present situation appeared novel, and their liberation almost incredible.

For two or three days, I was employed with strong fatigue parties, collecting the guns and caissons scattered on the roads, and among the fields to the north of the town. We dragged into park 174 cannon; of these, ninety were field pieces, all foul mouthed from recent use. The ground, for nearly a square league, was covered with the wreck of carriages, cars, chests, and baggage ; and, here and there, whole fields were literally white with thickly scattered papers. In their search for money and valuables, the soldiers had ransacked everything; they had torn out the lining of the carriages, and cut open the padding; they had broken all the correspondence chests of the various military and civil offices, and had strewn out papers, returns, and official documents, that had been, for years, perhaps, accumulating. You saw the finest military books and maps trod under foot, and utterly spoiled by the rain, that had fallen the day after the battle. In one part, very near a half destroyed *barouche*, I found a very interesting and beautiful letter, written in English, and addressed to his wife from Naples, by a Monsieur Thiebault; who, it appeared, had been treasurer to Joseph Buonaparte. With a little trouble, I discovered not less than twenty written by the same person, and in the same amiable and affectionate strain; they were dated from various places in Italy and Spain, and contained many natural and pleasing descriptions. I gathered them up, and returned home, rejoicing in my treasure. In the evening I went to a café, and seeing there several of the French officers taken, I asked one of them, if he knew a Monsieur Thiebault, the king's treasurer; he replied, extremely well, that he had been killed by a chance shot among the baggage on the 21st; that his son was a prisoner[19], and quite disconsolate; and that his wife, a most sweet

19. I made a packet of the letters, and sent them to the son, accompanied by a note, to which I did not sign my name, that he might not be distressed, by knowing or meeting one who had read this affectionate correspondence; and I had the happiness of learning, that the recovery of these papers, these precious memorials of an amiable parent, have proved the greatest consolation to this unhappy young man.

woman, and a native of Scotland, had left Vittoria for Bayonne on the 20th, and was still ignorant of her irreparable loss.

When the history of any individual, who has fallen, is thus brought before us, we feel deeply, but wander over ground, covered with corpses, about whom we know nothing, with comparative indifference; yet, if we knew the history attached to each lifeless body, on which we gazed, with what tales of sorrow should we not become acquainted. It would be, perhaps, difficult to select a more painful anecdote connected with the battle of Vittoria, than the following:—A paymaster of a regiment of British infantry had two sons, lieutenants in the corps in which he served; he was a widower, and had no relations besides these youths; they lived in his tent, were his pride and delight. The civil staff of a regiment usually remain with the baggage when the troops engage, and join them with it afterwards. In the evening, when this paymaster came up, an officer met him.

"My boys," said the old man, "how are they? Have they done their duty?"

"They have behaved most nobly; but you have lost—"

"Which of them?"

"Alas! both: they are numbered with the dead."

If this page should meet the eye of a man visited with affliction, let him think how heavily the arrows of misfortune lighted upon this grey head, and be resigned.

A friend of mine, belonging to another corps, lay wounded in Vittoria. I heard of it, and hastened to his billet. I found him reclining on a sofa, and looking, as I thought, remarkably well. He received me cordially and cheerfully. "I rejoice," said I, "to see you smiling; your injury is of course slight."

"You are mistaken; my wound is mortal, and my hours, I believe, are almost numbered. I shall never leave this room but as a corpse; but these are events which should never take a soldier by surprise."

With him the hurry and excitement of the conquered field had been exchanged for the calm, the awful calm of the chamber of death: he had been but yesterday in the season of his youth,

179

his strength and his hope; he was now gazing steadily upon, and advancing towards his grave. He died in two days. I saw him laid in the garden of a convent. Returning from his funeral I met a serjeant of my regiment, who had come with an escort from the division. "How are they all, serjeant?" said I.

"We have lost Mr. ———."

"How? In an affair?"—

"No; we had a dreadful storm among the mountains, and in one of the narrowest passes, himself and his horse were struck by lightning, and killed on the spot."

This too was a noble-minded zealous officer, one who had braved many a scene of peril, and whose ambition it had ever been to perish in the field. You grow familiar on service with death and sorrow; you do not weep—but if he have an eye to observe, and a heart to feel, few men see or suffer more than a soldier.

In Vittoria, I found an excellent bookseller's shop, and procured some of the classics, and the best French authors—Paris editions, and pocket-size, uncommonly cheap. This bookseller assured me that he had sold more books to the British in the course of one fortnight, than he had disposed of for two years to the French constantly passing through that city; and expressed great surprise, that among our officers so many reading men should be found.

It is certainly true, that in England the education of our military men appears, by comparison with those who study for the learned, professions, neglected and imperfect; but the British officers have better manners, more extensive information, and more cultivated minds, than those of any army in the world. I speak not of scientific attainments, for I believe the study of fortification, gunnery, and military mathematics, is more general with French and foreign officers than our own. One notion, however, is very prevalent in England about the French army, which is exceedingly erroneous. It is thought, that their marshals, their generals, and chiefs of the staff, are almost always mathematicians draughtsmen, men of science, and perfect tacticians, This is by no means the case. Zeal, intrepidity, ready intelligence, fearlessness under responsibility, and a practical acquaintance with war, are the qualities which have recommended, and lifted to honour and renown, the most distinguished officers of France, Genius directs, science obeys. The man of a daring and intelligent mind commands an army; the men of science labour, unseen, in the lower departments, and assist its operations. By their exertions, the face of a country is accurately mapped. Elevations and distances are correctly given; bridges are constructed, military roads traced up the pathless mountain, and fortresses breached; but, to decide upon the march, the assault, or the battle, belongs to the mind of a leader, to whom success with the compass and the pencil may have been denied; and, doubtless, abler draughtsmen, and abler mathematicians than themselves, have marched under the orders of a Wellington, and a Napoleon.

CHAPTER 16

The Fateful Pass at Maya

On the 5th of July, the detachments of our division marched to rejoin the army. I must not leave Vittoria without remarking, that it is a very clean town, has a very handsome square, excellent houses, good shops, and a well supplied market. The complexion of the inhabitants was much fairer than any I had before seen; some of the women, indeed, had blue eyes, and the brown hair and healthful cheek of our own countrywomen; which is not surprising, for the climate is cool and pleasant. The country, which we traversed, to Pampeluna, has a bold and interesting character. You are constantly moving through defiles and amid mountains. In the neighbourhood of the villages, the eye rests with pleasure on vineyards and corn-fields, overhanging each other on the sloping sides of the loftiest heights, and streams and rivulets sparkle all around.

In a village about three leagues from Pampeluna, where I passed the night, I met with a very fine man, a native of Arragon, and a guerilla. He was wounded in the leg, and of course for a time incapable of service. The circumstances of his situation, the fate of his family, and his language, will explain the nature both of the formation and feelings of many of these guerilla corps, better, perhaps, than a far longer and more detailed account of them. I asked him where he lived, and under whom he served.

"*Señor*," said he, "I have no home, no relations, nothing save my country and my sword. My father was led out, and shot in the market-place of my native village; our cottage was burned, my mother died of grief, and my wife, who had been violated by the enemy, fled to me, then a volunteer with Palafox, and died in my arms, in a hospital in Saragossa. I serve under no particular chief. I am too miserable, I feel too revengeful to support the restraint of discipline and the delay of manoeuvre. I go on any enterprise I hear of; if I am poor, on foot; if chance or plunder has made me rich, on horseback; I follow the boldest leader; but I have sworn never to dress a vine or plough a field till the enemy is driven out of Spain."

Such was the desperate, the undying hatred to the French which many of these guerillas cherished—a hatred which often had its source in wrongs and losses like those I have related, I have often heard my prejudiced country-men speak of these guerillas as irregular and lawless *banditti*, who only fought for, and who subsisted on, plunder. It is true they did subsist on plunder, but it was the plunder of their enemies. They were not paid, and could not live without support. Feelings, deadly feelings of revenge, drove them to exchange the plough and the pruning hook for the sword and the lance; and as their free and haughty spirits rejected the idea of serving in the ranks as soldiers, in no way could they give up their time to war, but by plundering where they conquered.

At the time I passed Pampeluna, it was blockaded by our troops. It is the chief city of Navarre, and one of the finest and most perfect fortresses in Spain. The road by which our detachments filed towards Villa Alba, ran along the face of a height within one mile of the place, and commanding a fine view both of the city and works. It was a summer afternoon; there was no stir, no bustle, no firing; it was a scene of still life. There is something infinitely grand in that air of stern repose and warlike security, which hangs over the grey walls of a formidable fortress, round which blockading foes lie idly in their scattered camps, and attempt nothing. Such was the aspect of Pampeluna: it frowned defiance, and was to be starved into submission. I looked with uncommon interest upon this scene. Groups of people were promenading the walls. Female figures leaning from the balconies; French soldiers lay indolently stretched out on the glacis, and on the grass near them cattle were feeding, while the sound of the convent and church bells conveyed the idea of profound peacefulness.

In my billet a little beyond Villa Alba, I met with excellent treatment, and my host presented me with some fine wine, of a tawny forbidding colour, but of most exquisite flavour. Our route from hence to Ortiz was singularly beautiful. There is a constant succession of verdant fertile valleys. Hedges of myrtle, and a fine clear stream, whose banks are all gaily and wildly decked with shrubs and flowers, give them a most rural and romantic character. It was painful, however, to see, that wherever in the space, on either side of the road, the ground had been flat and covered with corn, all was trodden down by the march of the, retiring French army. Between Ortiz and Lanz, the scenery is fine, and you pass a most magnificent forest of oaks. From Lanz to Berroeta the road, which is difficult and rocky, ascends a lofty mountain, so lofty, indeed, that Barretti says it is full as high as Mount Cenis.

We were three hours descending to Berroeta, by a narrow and broken road, by which, however, soma Portuguese artillery, under the direction of a most active and intelligent officer, did contrive to pass. When this was reported to the French officers, they were perfectly, incredulous, declaring that they had viewed that road as altogether impassable for guns. At Berroeta we entered the beautiful vale of Elizondo, or, as it is often called, San Estenan. It extends about two leagues and a half, and is bounded to the north by the Lower Pyrenees, which rise just above the village of Maya. The vale itself is so elevated that you are, perhaps, rather disappointed at first, by the appearance of the mountains which surround you. They are, indeed, bold and grand, and their sides are intersected by numberless wild and rugged ravines; some of them, too, have crests of grey and jagged rock; yet, again, the tops of many are round, smooth, and verdant, and seem to invite ascent.

We passed through the small town of Elizondo, where the

head-quarters of Lord Hill were established; through that of Maya, the division head-quarters; and striking off here to the right, with a guide sent from the regiment, I pursued the path with my detachment towards a lofty mountain, on the very summit of which I discerned the white tents of my corps, like small flakes of snow lying still unmelted on its top. I had now done with roads and villages. The face of the country grew bolder every step. We moved up a path so perpendicular and rocky, that it was wonderful how a mule with any burthen could make its way. For two hours and a half we toiled and toiled, till at length the greeting shout of our comrades, who crowded round us with welcoming hands and voices, told us, that rough and rugged as were these mountain-wilds, they contained for us a home. I was not allowed a moment's repose. Two companions caught me by the hands, and hurrying me forward to an elevated spot a few hundred yards in front of our encampment, bade me, as a reward for my fatiguing march, look on the scene below me; and what a scene of loveliness, cultivation, and verdure! France lay stretched out beneath us; our view was only bounded by the horizon. From the point at which we stood, the arid and sandy deserts of the Landes were hid from us by a fine screen of mountain, while the lovely plains of southern France, all carpeted with corn and pasture, woods and vineyards, lay spread before us, finely contrasting their rich produce and smiling villages with the air of desolation, loneliness, and grandeur, that reigned more immediately around us; for here the chain of the Pyrenees was in part discoverable. To the right, lofty peaks, white with the snows of ages, bold and varied in their forms, and with hues ever changing, as the light or shadow rested on them, rose above each other in rude majesty. Never was a nobler barrier placed between two nations by the hand of Heaven, than this chain of the Pyrenees, against whose western point, the rough and restless waters of the Bay of Biscay are ever fiercely beating: while the Mediterranean gently washes the feet of its eastern cliffs.

It is true these mountains are not so lofty as the Alps; Mount Perdu, the highest of them, not being quite 12,000 feet above the level of the sea. But, like the Alps, they have their glaciers, their icy caverns; like them are subject to the avalanche; and, doubtless, all the wonders of nature, which have so charmed the visitors of Alpine scenery, would be met with in the central and eastern Pyrenees, were they as carefully explored. Our camp lay full seven thousand feet above the level of the sea, but was quite free from snow, except here and there in some clefts a few patches remained; nor were we, except towards the dawn of morning, at all incommoded by cold. The corps presented here a very novel appearance. From the great want of shoes, many of the men had been provided with the light hempen sandal, made and worn by the natives of this province, and well adapted to the steep and slippery heights by which they are surrounded; the becoming cap, too, of these mountaineers, was quite the fashion with our officers. But the natural grace and agility of the finely-formed race of men who inhabit these mountain-vales, are not to be acquired by him who has been born in cities, and nurtured on the plain. Their light step in ascending the loftiest mountains, their activity in leaping from one fragment of rock to another, as they cross the wild ravines and tumbling torrents which often intercept their path, and the secure, yet fearless rapidity of their course down the most dangerous steeps, are truly astonishing to the eye of a stranger.

From the vale of Elizondo there is a pass which leads by Maya, through the village of Urdaz, into France; and there are three mountain-paths on the right, called the Puertas de Ariete, Espegue, and Lareta. With the defence of the Espegue pass our corps was charged when I joined; and in a spot, about half a mile from our camp, we daily mounted a strong picquet I shall never forget the rude path which led to it, or the happy day I passed there; the dash of torrents and the scream of eagles were the only sounds heard in that wild region. At times, the picturesque figure of one of the herdsmen or hunters of those solitudes was seen hurrying past, who smiled on and saluted us. How wonderfully hath Providence ordered our desires, when it can make the mountaineer look from his barren portion of rock and snow, upon the golden vales beneath him without a sigh, and live contentedly a life of peril: and privation, while one of comparative ease and plenty is offered to his choice; and thus it is with us all. He who has a cultivated mind and a rich imagination delights to travel, and store his mind with images, the recollection of which may brighten his hours of retirement and reflection; but ask the Englishman, as he climbs the Alps, gazes on the Rhine, pauses amid the ruins of ancient Rome, or views the splendid scenery of the Bay of Naples,—ask him if he will become a dweller in any of these countries for ever— these countries, rich in scenes which he contemplates with enthusiasm, and for which, in his own gloomy climate, he may look in vain:— he would laugh at the simplicity of the question. No; the same power, which has allotted such smiling paths of creation to others, has girt in his own precious country with rock and sea; and has, by a thousand advantages, endeared to him a land, from the tame scenery and clouded atmosphere of which, the natives of romantic Switzerland and brilliant Italy would turn aside, almost with a feeling of disgust.

In a very few days, my regiment changed its ground for a bivouack in front of the village of Maya. As we wound down the mountain, a friend told me an anecdote of Spanish courage, which I have pleasure in recording. In a skirmish with the enemy, on the 7th of July, he observed, that a peasant, armed only with a horse pistol, had introduced himself among his skirmishers; seeing that the pistol could not possibly take effect, he thanked him, praised him for his courage, but advised him to go away.

"*Mas cerca puedo matar?*" (Can I kill nearer?) said the man eagerly.   ·

"*Si,*" said my friend, smiling. The man immediately ran considerably in front of the line of skirmishers, fired, returned to load again, went forward, and continued so to fight in company with our men; escaping, I rejoice to add, unhurt. To this anecdote, I may add one of British generosity of sentiment: I heard a section of our men speaking in terms of great admiration of the gallantry of a French officer, who, it seems, had made himself very conspicuous in a late skirmish in trying to bring on his men.

"I was sorry to see him drop, poor fellow," said one.

"Ah!" said another, " he came so close there was no missing him; I did for him!"

"Did you!" rejoined the first speaker; "by God, I could not have pulled a trigger at him. No; damn me, I like fair fighting and hot fighting; but I could not single out such a man in cold blood."

My regiment and the brigade now lay bivouacked, for some time, in rear of the Maya heights; and a steep and toilsome ascent of two miles and a half separated us from that part of the heights, with the defence of which we were charged, and on which we daily mounted a picquet of eighty men. About one mile in rear of the picquet post lay the light companies of the brigade, as a post of communication and a support.

On the 25th of July, the enemy attacked and carried the pass of Maya with an overwhelming force. It was a day of brave confusion. It was a surprise, and it was not a surprise. It was one, because the nature of the country favoured the near approach and concealed advance of large bodies of the enemy; and the troops who were destined to defend the right of these heights were two miles and a half distant, and had not time to arrive and form. Only one regiment, in fact, arriving at all in sufficient time to fight on the important ground; and this corps, breathless with exertion, and engaging by groups, as they came up. Again, it was not a surprise, because no affair was ever more regularly opened and contested by the picquet and light companies, than that of the 25th of July. It was not a day to be easily forgotten by me, for it threw me into the hands of the enemy, and disappointed me of the honour of marching under British colours, fearlessly, nay, triumphantly, displayed into some of the finest provinces of southern France. Such a day of my life I shall give as one of strange recollections.

It was a pleasant arbour on the banks of a mountain-stream,

that I breakfasted on that very morning (aye, and I well remember, with a volume of the *Rambler* for a companion). At seven o'clock, I relieved the picquet on the Maya Heights, and learned from the captain of it, that he had seen a group of horse and a column of troops, pass along the face of a distant hill, at dawn, and disappear. I requested him to make a special report of this when he reached the camp, which he did. A deputy quartermaster general came up soon after; rode a little in front, said, that there was, indeed, a small column discernible about three miles off in a vale, but that it was only a change of bivouack, or some trifling movement of no consequence.

I thought otherwise, and the event proved I was not mistaken. The light companies were, indeed, ordered up by this officer, as a measure of precaution: how very weak and insufficient a one, will be seen. In less than two hours, my picquet and the light companies were heavily engaged with the enemy's advance, which was composed entirely of voltigeur companies, unencumbered by knapsacks, and led by a chosen officer. These fellows fought with ardour, but we disputed our ground with them handsomely, and caused them severe loss; nor had we lost the position itself, though driven from the advances of it, when joined by the hastily arriving groups of the right corps of our brigade, (my own regiment.)

The enemy's numbers now, however, increased every moment; they covered the country immediately in front of, and around, us. The sinuosities of the mountains, the ravines, the water-courses, were filled with their advancing and overwhelming force.

The contest now, if contest it could be called, was very unequal; and, of course, short and bloody. I saw two-thirds of my picquet, and numbers, both of the light companies and my own regiment, destroyed. Among other brave victims, our captain of grenadiers nobly fell, covered with wounds; our colonel desperately wounded, and many others; and surviving this carnage, was myself made prisoner. I owe the preservation of a life, about which I felt, in that irritating moment, regardless, to the interference of a French officer, who beat up the muskets of his leading section, already levelled for my destruction; which must, (for I was within six or seven paces of them,) have annihilated me. This noble fellow, with some speech about "*un François sait respecter les braves*," embraced me, and bade an orderly conduct me to Count D'Erlon.

The column by which I was taken was composed of the 8th and 75th Regiments of the French line. Good God! how sudden a change! A minute before I had been uttering, and listening to the cry of "forward;" now I heard all around me "*en avant*," "*en avant*," "*vive Napoléon*," "*vive l'Empereur*."

I was in the midst of these men; they passed me hurried, and roughly. None insulted, none attempted to plunder me. But in a ravine, full of rascally sculking stragglers, who are always the cowards and plunderers of an army, I was robbed by the very fellow, who, willing to leave the fight, had volunteered to conduct me. The appearance of some slightly-wounded men returning from the front, and of a serjeant-major, caused him to run off with his booty, and by the serjeant-major I was conducted to Count D'Erlon, who was on horseback, on a commanding height near, surrounded by a large group of staff officers.

"*Un capitaine Anglois, général*," said my conductor. The count took off his hat instantly, and spoke to me in a manner the most delicate, and the most flattering, asking no questions, but complimenting highly the brave resistance which had been offered to him.

It was a strange scene—French faces and uniforms all around me; and two columns of his reserve halted just behind him. They were not here disarmed, ragged, looking spiritless, or affecting misplaced gaiety. Their clothing was nearly new, their appointments excellent, and their whole appearance clean, steady, and soldier-like.

One of the officers of the count's staff dismounted, and offered me "*la goutte*" from his leathern bottle, which I declined. The enemy suffered severely; slightly-wounded men were passing every minute, and on the face of the heights lay very many of the killed and severely wounded. Small parties of the English prisoners, too, might be seen bringing in from the left of the Maya Heights, and from the rear, where they still contended in a brave, disjointed manner, without support. The count soon dismissed me, saying he had no horse to offer me, but that the town whither he had ordered the prisoners was not very distant; and, turning to the serjeant-major, he bade him conduct himself towards the English officers taken, (for two others were brought up while I was with him) as he would to Frenchmen of the same rank.

In the rear of the column of reserve, all the English taken were collected; and here I met a brother officer, a lieutenant of our light company, who had much distinguished himself throughout the day, and was taken in another part of the field, and not many minutes after my capture. He was my most intimate and valued friend, and meeting him under such circumstances overcame me. I shed tears.

"*Regardez donc,*" said a vulgar-looking French officer, who was observing us, "*regardez comme ils sont des enfans ces Anglois; ils pleurent.*"

"*Ah, mon ami,*" said his companion, "*vous ne connoissez pas les Anglois: ce ne sont pas les larmes de l'enfance qu'ils versent.*"

Our party now set forward, conducted and followed by but few; for as there was no possibility of escape, we were guided rather than escorted. There were 140 English in all, but not more than forty of any one regiment, and only four officers. As we passed along, we met more French troops coming up along the narrow mountain road. None of the soldiers offered to insult us; many of the officers indeed saluted us, though here and there a decorated officer smoothed his *moustachios* as he looked upon us, with an air of impatient *brusquerie*. It was quite amusing to see the rapidity with which a lie had been framed, and passed down their files. Myself, and one of the officers taken as battalion of-ficers, wore epaulettes of bullion. As the leading sections of this French brigade passed us, we heard them say, "*deux chefs de ba-taillon prisonniers;*" but, as the rear came up, they were crying out "*en avant,*" "*l'affaire va bien*"—"*deux bataillons prises aux ennemis.*"

It was in vain I said *"Je ne suis que capitaine;"*
Still the cry ran, *"vive Napoléon,"*
"deux bataillons prises aux ennemis."—
"Battre une fois ces Anglois ce seroit un plaisir," muttered an elderly looking, hard featured colonel, as he passed us, bowing gravely, unconscious, no doubt, that we understood this negative acknowledgement of our past and repeated successes.

LEONAUR

ALSO FROM LEONAUR
AVAILABLE IN SOFTCOVER OR HARDCOVER WITH DUST JACKET

THE JENA CAMPAIGN: 1806 by F. N. Maude—The Twin Battles of Jena & Auerstadt Between Napoleon's French and the Prussian Army.

PRIVATE O'NEIL by Charles O'Neil—The recollections of an Irish Rogue of H. M. 28th Regt.—The Slashers— during the Peninsula & Waterloo campaigns of the Napoleonic wars.

ROYAL HIGHLANDER by James Anton—A soldier of H.M 42nd (Royal) Highlanders during the Peninsular, South of France & Waterloo Campaigns of the Napoleonic Wars.

CAPTAIN BLAZE by Elzéar Blaze—Elzéar Blaze recounts his life and experiences in Napoleon's army in a well written, articulate and companionable style.

LEJEUNE VOLUME 1 by Louis-François Lejeune—The Napoleonic Wars through the Experiences of an Officer on Berthier's Staff.

LEJEUNE VOLUME 2 by Louis-François Lejeune—The Napoleonic Wars through the Experiences of an Officer on Berthier's Staff.

FUSILIER COOPER by John S. Cooper—Experiences in the 7th (Royal) Fusiliers During the Peninsular Campaign of the Napoleonic Wars and the American Campaign to New Orleans.

CAPTAIN COIGNET by Jean-Roch Coignet—A Soldier of Napoleon's Imperial Guard from the Italian Campaign to Russia and Waterloo.

FIGHTING NAPOLEON'S EMPIRE by Joseph Anderson—The Campaigns of a British Infantryman in Italy, Egypt, the Peninsular & the West Indies During the Napoleonic Wars.

CHASSEUR BARRES by Jean-Baptiste Barres—The experiences of a French Infantryman of the Imperial Guard at Austerlitz, Jena, Eylau, Friedland, in the Peninsular, Lutzen, Bautzen, Zinnwald and Hanau during the Napoleonic Wars.

MARINES TO 95TH (RIFLES) by Thomas Fernyhough—The military experiences of Robert Fernyhough during the Napoleonic Wars.

HUSSAR ROCCA by Albert Jean Michel de Rocca—A French cavalry officer's experiences of the Napoleonic Wars and his views on the Peninsular Campaigns against the Spanish, British And Guerilla Armies.

SERGEANT BOURGOGNE by Adrien Bourgogne—With Napoleon's Imperial Guard in the Russian Campaign and on the Retreat from Moscow 1812 - 13.

LEONAUR

ALSO FROM LEONAUR
AVAILABLE IN SOFTCOVER OR HARDCOVER WITH DUST JACKET

WELLINGTON AND THE PYRENEES CAMPAIGN VOLUME I: FROM VITORIA TO THE BIDASSOA *by F. C. Beatson*—The final phase of the campaign in the Iberian Peninsula.

WELLINGTON AND THE INVASION OF FRANCE VOLUME II: THE BIDASSOA TO THE BATTLE OF THE NIVELLE *by F. C. Beatson*—The second of Beatson's series on the fall of Revolutionary France published by Leonaur, the reader is once again taken into the centre of Wellington's strategic and tactical genius.

WELLINGTON AND THE FALL OF FRANCE VOLUME III: THE GAVES AND THE BATTLE OF ORTHEZ *by F. C. Beatson*—This final chapter of F. C. Beatson's brilliant trilogy shows the 'captain of the age' at his most inspired and makes all three books essential additions to any Peninsular War library.

NAVAL BATTLES OF THE NAPOLEONIC WARS *by W. H. Fitchett*—Cape St. Vincent, the Nile, Cadiz, Copenhagen, Trafalgar & Others

SERGEANT GUILLEMARD: THE MAN WHO SHOT NELSON? *by Robert Guillemard*—A Soldier of the Infantry of the French Army of Napoleon on Campaign Throughout Europe

WITH THE GUARDS ACROSS THE PYRENEES *by Robert Batty*—The Experiences of a British Officer of Wellington's Army During the Battles for the Fall of Napoleonic France, 1813.

A STAFF OFFICER IN THE PENINSULA *by E. W. Buckham*—An Officer of the British Staff Corps Cavalry During the Peninsula Campaign of the Napoleonic Wars

THE LEIPZIG CAMPAIGN: 1813—NAPOLEON AND THE "BATTLE OF THE NATIONS" *by F. N. Maude*—Colonel Maude's analysis of Napoleon's campaign of 1813.

BUGEAUD: A PACK WITH A BATON by *Thomas Robert Bugeaud*—The Early Campaigns of a Soldier of Napoleon's Army Who Would Become a Marshal of France.

TWO LEONAUR ORIGINALS

SERGEANT NICOL by *Daniel Nicol*—The Experiences of a Gordon Highlander During the Napoleonic Wars in Egypt, the Peninsula and France.

WATERLOO RECOLLECTIONS by *Frederick Llewellyn*—Rare First Hand Accounts, Letters, Reports and Retellings from the Campaign of 1815.